The HOT SEAT

The HOT SEAT

A YEAR OF OUTRAGE, PRIDE, AND OCCASIONAL GAMES OF COLLEGE FOOTBALL

BEN MATHIS-LILLEY

PublicAffairs
New York

PublicAffairs
Hachette Book Group
1290 Avenue of the Americas, New York, NY 10104
www.publicaffairsbooks.com
@Public_Affairs

Printed in the United States of America

First Edition: August 2022

Published by PublicAffairs, an imprint of Perseus Books, LLC, a subsidiary of Hachette Book Group, Inc. The PublicAffairs name and logo is a trademark of the Hachette Book Group.

The Hachette Speakers Bureau provides a wide range of authors for speaking events. To find out more, go to www.hachettespeakersbureau.com or call (866) 376-6591.

The publisher is not responsible for websites (or their content) that are not owned by the publisher.

Library of Congress Cataloging-in-Publication Data has been applied for.

ISBNs: 9781541700338 (hardcover), 9781541700352 (ebook)

LSC-C

Printing 1, 2022

CONTENTS

To the ten year olds playing
"The Victors," past and future

CHAPTER

1

I'VE NEVER FELT THIS BAD

AT ABOUT 1:50 p.m. EST on Saturday, November 7, 2020, a lot of people were thinking about the United States presidential election. Just before noon, a number of news outlets had projected that Joe Biden would win the state of Pennsylvania, making him the presumed next president after four tense days of waiting for votes to be counted.

I was supposed to be one of those people. My job is to write about the news for the online news magazine *Slate*, and the 2020 American presidential election was a pretty big news story. Instead, the record shows that at that time, on that day, I was sending an email, the subject line of which was "Next Coach Thread," to five other people.

The University of Michigan football team was in the process of losing to the historically mediocre Indiana University football team and falling to a record of 1-2 with a number of additional losses presumed to be imminent. I felt it was important as "an act of formally moving on"—those are my exact, still-embarrassing words—to begin discussing who might become the team's head coach after its current coach, the zealously unconventional Jim Harbaugh, was dismissed, which I assumed to be an inevitability. The six of us on the email chain are citizens of a country that was at that moment experiencing unprecedented electoral chaos. We have a combined six spouses, six mortgages, and eleven children— in other words, a lot of other things to think about. We exchanged thirty-seven more messages about Michigan's football coaching situation over the next forty-eight hours. (I did some posts about the election for my real job too.)

The season only got worse, and the group conversations became more heated. Here are some highlights from another 2020 Michigan football discussion that I was part of, this one conducted via Twitter direct messages with an entirely different group of people, none of whom I had ever met, at that point, in real life:

- "This is a catastrophe for the entire Harbaugh Era"
- "Harbaugh's worst loss"
- "I've never been more OK firing Harbaugh"
- "Worst loss of the Harbaugh Era and it's not that close"
- "[name of player] needs to be sent to space jail"
- "I'm gonna kill my self [sic] in real life" [he was joking; he's still alive]
- "this team is not good fellas"
- "we suck lmao"
- "This is a paradigm shifting loss"
- "I've never felt this bad"
- "I've learned the most important lesson in life: it sucks"
- "There is no more fun to be had for me"
- "With every succeeding snap my belief in firing him on the spot grows"

- "Basically anything would be an improvement over this"
- "it particularly sucks to see all these guys who can play put in a position to suck donkey ass"
- "OK gang give me a few hours. I'm gonna fly to Ann Arbor Municipal Airport, and then I'm gonna pick up Jim Harbaugh. And then I'm gonna drive him back to the airport so we can fire him on the tarmac"
- "It really is like they have eight players on the field"
- "This is worse than would've been reasonable to expect. And it would've been reasonable to expect bad"
- "It seems like we have six guys on the field"
- "guys what the fuck"
- "please quit your job jim"
- "soup soup soup soup soup soup soup soup soup soup soup soup soup soup soup soup soup soup soup soup soup soup soup soup"
  [The coach that many people wanted Michigan to hire to replace Harbaugh was Iowa State's Matt *Campbell*, hence "soup."]
- "I keep saying this and it's not rhetorical: What is this team doing in practice"
- "God dude"
- "That was awful"
- "So bad"
- "dflksdjfklsdjf"
- "The moon landing didn't happen"

I'm not sure what that last one was in reference to. But the word *fire* comes up 293 times in an archive of messages from that fall. We did not all necessarily feel personal hostility toward Jim Harbaugh. Some did, while some felt sad for him. But we all assumed that he was not going to be the coach of the Michigan football team anymore and that he had earned that fate.

Many, many other people felt the same way. On the MGoBlog fan site, the subject of discussion in the comments section under a recap of the Wolverines' 49-11 November loss to Wisconsin—its worst home loss in eighty-five years—was not whether Harbaugh should be fired, but who else the university should fire such that "the root cause of the systemic suck is figured out and eliminated." The word *fuck* appeared 171 times in comments about the game. (One of the site's moderators tracks this figure each week.)

Harbaugh was described as on the verge of being canned—or assumed to be a foregone subject of termination—by sportswriters and commentators at the Associated Press, CBS, Fox Sports, and multiple arms of the ESPN content machine. (ESPN had also asserted that his job was in danger in 2019, while Yahoo! Sports and Fox had done so in 2018.) Later in November, Michigan was beaten by a COVID-19–addled Penn State team that at that point was 0-5 and whose signature move was fumbling the ball. On Twitter, ABC color analyst Brian Griese, a professionally objective and even-tempered observer who, like Harbaugh, is a former Big Ten champion Michigan quarterback, posted a graphic highlighting the low points of the coach's recent record with the caption "enough is enough." National sportswriters and pundits made jokes and exchanged memes at Michigan's expense, of the sort that suggested other football teams in the Big Ten conference would be so happy to see Harbaugh retained as coach that they would dance in the manner of characters from popular film and television programs.

Multiple people with connections to the Michigan program to whom I've spoken identified the team's October home loss to Michigan State University Spartans, which preceded the Indiana game, as the most shockingly grim of the 2020 season's many grim events. MSU, naturally one of Michigan's biggest rivals, was playing with a roster that had been thinned out during a transition between head coaches and had lost its previous game to Rutgers, which is generally not a good team. MSU nonetheless beat Michigan 27-24 on its own field. (Because of COVID-19, there was no crowd. Harbaugh wore a mask *over* his headset microphone all season, distending it to the point of both aesthetic and epidemiological unsoundness.) The margin of the final score belied both the game's horrible air of disaster and the simultaneously panicked and anesthetized manner in which the Michigan coaching staff seemed to have prepared the team to play. MSU basically had one offensive idea, which was throwing the ball as high up in the air as possible and hoping that someone on the right team would catch it, as is done at elementary schools. It worked every time. As one person I spoke to put it, "Jesus Christ."

Michigan finished the season 2-4, with six games canceled because of COVID-19.

The coach of a college football team can make thousands, hundreds of thousands, and perhaps even millions of people—many of them otherwise stable and superficially reasonable adults—insanely angry. I experience churning gastrointestinal distress on Saturdays during the season until Michigan has a lead of at least seventeen points. In my idle moments, when taking showers and driving my three children around northern New Jersey, I spend more time mentally debating self-posed hypotheses such as, "Did Jim Harbaugh corner himself into a no-man's land between the Wisconsin/Iowa system development model and the Ohio/Penn State talent acquisition model?" than I do thinking about any other question, including things such as, "Do I have the right career?" and "What are parents' and children's obligations to each other?" and "What happens to our souls when our bodies die?" This kind of fixation, conducive to neither peace of mind nor personal productivity, is very common.

Why are so many people like this?

CHAPTER

2

THE HOT SEAT

THE QUESTION OF WHETHER it is absurd and undesirable to care to the point of physical discomfort about sports has nagged at me for some time. I was also deeply bothered for several recent years by the question of why Jim Harbaugh had not been more successful as Michigan's coach and whether he should be fired.

The roots of these preoccupations extend back to the 1980s and 1990s, when my family lived about one hundred miles north of Ann Arbor. (The town I was raised in, Midland, is a city-sized Dow Chemical plant to which houses and a school district have been attached for convenience.) Sometime around 1990, at the age of eightish, I became a Michigan football fan. My parents weren't natives of the state and no longer live there, and while they both like sports, I think they find my level of interest in the team a little weird. I didn't go to college at U of M, but I liked the colors on the uniforms, I liked the big stadium and the marching band, I liked when players ran with or caught the ball for touchdowns, and I liked that Michigan usually won. So that was that. Go Blue!

About a dozen years ago, I read a book about soccer called *Football Against the Enemy*, which observed that the way the sport was played in different countries—down to what happened on the field, in terms of strategy and style—varied because of historical and cultural factors particular to each place. This struck me as a mind-blowing framework to apply to college football. By its nature, NCAA football is not as well played as NFL football, but there is still something about this version of the sport that many people find compelling to the point of madness. Perhaps this is because college games are contests not just between teams and players but between ways of life.

In US professional sports, athletes who only rarely have a personal connection to their team's home city perform in generic corporate arenas, team operations overseen by an MBA class that treats wins and losses as data points in a process of asset maximization. But in college football, teams have many of the characteristics of the places where they play. Rosters, even on the most nationally dominant teams, are disproportionately built from local and regional high schools. Programs often maintain trademark styles for generations. The things I and others are drawn to—the colors, the crowds, the chants, the rivalries—are not just matters of marketing (though they are definitely also that) but of personal and communal identity.

There are some instincts and urges that explain the appeal of sports in general to humans, like the attraction to physical spectacle and the compulsion to find out the ending (i.e., final score) of a given story (i.e., game). These become more powerful when they intersect with the equally ancient tendency to think of oneself and one's social group in reference to epic narratives and heroes. In the United States, no sport plays more obviously to that tendency—projecting the message that the people on the field represent the particular people watching from the stands or on TV—than college football. As *Sports Illustrated*'s Richard Johnson said to me, "College football makes people in New York City think about what people in Oxford, Mississippi, and Tuscaloosa, Alabama, are interested in." If you go somewhere new in the United States and want to know what makes it different from other places, the fastest way to do that might be to observe its preeminent college team.

For example, at the time I read *Football Against the Enemy*, the University of Oregon—based in fast-growing Eugene, its program funded in large part by Nike billionaire Phil Knight—was running elaborate misdirection plays at an unprecedented, no-huddle speed and attaching GPS trackers to players during practice. Louisiana State, playing in Baton Rouge among alligators and swamp vegetation, ran the ball up the middle most of the time, using plays that were many decades old, with straightforward and brutal intentions. The team's coach sometimes ate grass off of the field during games as a self-invented folk treatment; he said it helped keep him humble. Both teams were excellent. Both approaches worked!

Nowhere are college football identities expressed more conspicuously than through the head coach. Coaches must not only win but also exemplify the sometimes contradictory values and ideals that supporters believe their schools and teams stand for (e.g., unrelenting dominance, but also widely appreciated integrity). Their job security is ultimately determined by fans who have, on the one hand, extremely unreasonable expectations and, on the other hand, only the vaguest idea why teams ultimately succeed or fail.

If a coach isn't winning decisively every year, it is understood that he is on the hot seat. This means he is being attacked by alumni, former players, big-money donors, TV pundits, and online cranks who believe he should be fired. After every loss, social media sites, message boards, radio airwaves, and podcasts—my God, the podcasts—will be overloaded with opinions about how he is, to take one time-honored binary, either calling too many passes (because "games are won or lost in the trenches") or not calling enough passes (because "you've got to adapt to modern football"). A coach is never more than a few high-stakes victories from having a statue built in his honor while he's still alive. But he is also never more than one defeat from turning into a widely derided idiot whose face becomes a meme image that young people use to signify failure. (In 2016, Texas Christian really did erect a statue of its then coach, Gary Patterson, on campus. In 2021, Patterson resigned under pressure because of the team's poor record.) The coach exists in a state of perpetual water-cooler subjecthood.

Coaches, for all their belief in self-reliance and the determinative power of "wanting it more than the other guy," are at the mercy of trends and conditions over which they have no control. These are numerous and involved, ranging from the decentralized structure of US higher education (which requires colleges to continually pursue more money and prestige or risk ceasing to exist), to the decline of industry in the Midwest (which has drastically changed the distribution of football talent), to media corporations' decisions about what will maximize their advertising revenue (which leads to reorganizations of college football's competitive environment on an almost annual basis).

The sport can be a little too revealing about who "we" are. When a friend of mine who did not attend a "football school" mentioned that his general impression of the college game was one of overinvested psycho fans, sleazy boosters, exploitative corporate sponsors, and coaches who alternate between being psychologically abusive and legally overpermissive, the only thing I could say was, well, yeah. It's a sport that has seemed unsustainably chaotic at every stage of its existence, and now it seems especially so. For many years, colleges have withheld revenue from the players who are generating it on the principle that they are "student-athletes" playing an amateur sport for nonpecuniary reasons, even though that amateur sport is worth billions of dollars and the students recruited to play it are all but excluded from the normal activities of collegiate life, lest they take time or attention away from football.

This pretense, thin and transparent in the best of times, is finally beginning to disappear in practice, most prominently via the adoption of the "name, image, and likeness" (NIL) rights that allow NCAA athletes to accept sports-related income so long as it doesn't come from schools themselves. More players are sharing their feelings about political questions, and not just those that are related to amateurism and compensation. Some fans like this. Others really don't!

This book is an account of one season of football, the many swear words said aloud and written on the internet about it, and some guesses as to why those words felt so important to the people delivering them. In particular, it examines the reputations of a few head coaches who were in precarious positions within this crazed environment. Chief among these is Harbaugh, the subject whom I felt I was most suited to investigate and explain as both a journalistic observer and a demented fan. I also took a trip to study Ed Orgeron, the bayou-born coach of the Louisiana State University Tigers, another team with a storied history and huge stadium, but one that is unencumbered, both for better and for worse, by Michigan's pretension and sense of propriety. And I went to Florida to see Willie Taggart, who had been an up-and-coming star when he was named head coach of Florida State University in 2017 but was fired by FSU less than two years later. As of this writing, he is working at Florida Atlantic University, an erstwhile commuter school in Boca Raton. My hope was that by figuring out why these men had troubles with their job security, and by interspersing my scrutiny of Michigan with trips to places that were very much not-Michigan, I would be able to learn more about both the forces that created the wider college football universe and Michigan's place within that cosmos. Perhaps, by understanding the hot seat, we can understand ourselves.

CHAPTER
3

HOPE-O-METER

"THICC STAUSKAS" had seen enough. It was August 23, 2021, twelve days before Michigan was scheduled to begin its football season with a home game against Western Michigan University. The proximate trigger for his anger was an article on 247Sports .com's Michigan Insider website called *Webblog: Fall Camp Rumblings—Talking "Offensive Identity."* In the post, reporter Sam Webb (hence *Webb*log) wrote the following: "My gut tells me that the thing this offense is best at right now is when it's pounding the rock." The reference to Webb's "gut" is a code phrase that he uses to indicate that he has firsthand information.

To Thicc Stauskas—a 247Sports.com subscriber and Twitter user with about three thousand followers whose handle is a portmanteau involving former Michigan basketball player Nik Stauskas and the late-millennial slang term *thicc*, which means that someone's butt is big but in a good way—this was unacceptable and devastating. It was the exact thing he feared, expected, and hated. "It's over," he wrote on Twitter, referring to the season, which had not started. "I hate this shit!" On the 247Sports message board thread associated with Webb's post, he responded "this sucks," reiterating this belief several times in an extended argument with other users. Within about an hour, he was suspended from the site, ostensibly for posting some of the paywalled text from Webb's article elsewhere online but also, it seemed like, for being too mad. (He had additionally violated the site's prohibition on personal attacks forty-six minutes into the discussion by telling another user that he had "the brain of a tiny baby.")

This incident, in addition to being funny to me because I knew that "Thicc Stauskas" was an otherwise pretty normal person in his midtwenties named Dan, was illustrative of the mood that had surrounded the Michigan football program since the previous season, and for most of Jim Harbaugh's coaching tenure, and for most of the twenty-first century. (Dan—Thicc Stauskas—is one of the people in the Twitter message chat mentioned earlier.) The specific issue under dispute—the advisability of pounding the rock, that is, handing off to running backs rather than passing or using a "mobile" running quarterback—was itself central to Michigan's problem, which was the gap between its self-conception and its performance.

Michigan was a good-to-great football team for most of the modern, postintegration era of college football, which began in roughly 1970. The team's winningest coach during this or any time was Bo Schembechler, who assembled sizable young men with names like Rick, Billy, and Jumbo and believed strongly in running the ball—in 1973, Michigan ran 692 times and attempted only 102 passes.

The date the program's modern era of excellence ended can arguably be pinpointed to November 17, 2006, when Schembechler collapsed and died of a heart attack while preparing to record a TV segment in the Detroit suburb of Southfield. He was retired by then, but he had stayed close to the program and been followed in succession by two of his former assistants, including the coach at the time, Lloyd Carr. Carr's team was undefeated and preparing to play number-one-ranked rival Ohio State the next day. Michigan had won a national championship less than a decade prior—I was fifteen at the time; it was awesome—and a Big Ten championship as recently as 2003. One of its recent quarterbacks (Tom Brady) was in the beginning stages of becoming the most accomplished football player ever. Wide receiver and kick returner Desmond Howard had won the Heisman Trophy in 1992 (he was awesome), while cornerback/kick returner/wide receiver Charles Woodson had won it in 1997 (he was also awesome).

The day after Schembechler's death, the team lost narrowly to Ohio State. A month and a half later, it was beaten decisively by the University of Southern California in the Rose Bowl. It lost the first game of the next season, 2007, to Appalachian State, a woodsy North Carolina school whose team didn't even play at the Division I-A level at the time. It was the most shocking upset in college football history, and it remains so. (MGoBlog refers to this game as "The Horror.") Then, in its fourth straight loss, Michigan was pasted 39-7 at home by the University of Oregon Ducks. Both App State and Oregon succeeded by using players who were, on the whole, lighter, faster, and more creatively arranged around the field than Michigan's. This was not awesome, and two months later, Carr announced that he would step down at the season's end.

He was replaced by Rich "Rich Rod" Rodriguez, a native of West Virginia who'd had success as the head coach of West Virginia University with an offensive system largely of his own invention that, despite being mostly running-oriented, was considered novel because it used smaller and more spread-out players, including the quarterback, to carry the ball. Schembechler had used running quarterbacks initially, but over the course of his tenure and Carr's, the Michigan model for the position had mostly become a tall person who handed off a lot.

Rodriguez's teams were bad for myriad reasons that are blessedly beyond the scope of this book, but the lesson many Michigan partisans took from his tenure was that you could not win in the Big Ten if your running backs were not expected to plunge frequently into a centrally located pile of six to eleven opponents. Rich Rod was fired after three years and replaced by former Carr assistant Brady Hoke, a personable man who looks and sounds like Fred Flintstone. Hoke talked a lot about power running and "big-boy football," but his teams (after one good year mostly using Rodriguez's leftover plays) were bad in general and particularly bad at running the ball. Michigan rushed for negative forty-eight yards in a blowout loss to Michigan State in Hoke's third year as coach. That's not good, and it's certainly not powerful. He got fired.

This was when Harbaugh was brought in. He had been a quarterback at Michigan under Schembechler, had had a long NFL career, and had become a successful coach at Stanford University and then with the San Francisco 49ers. We'll delve into some other aspects of his character and the furor around his arrival later, but it was a big deal. Tom Brady, Desmond Howard, and then Michigan governor Rick Snyder reportedly were among those who personally urged him to take the job, which was pitched to him in clandestine phone conversations by interim Michigan athletic director (AD) Jim Hackett. Hackett would leave the university soon afterward to become CEO of Ford, and his pursuit of Harbaugh had the reported support of Michigan mega-donor Stephen Ross, who owns a number of entities, including the Equinox and SoulCycle gym brands, the Miami Dolphins, and the Related Companies real estate firm. (Ross has given more to the university than any other person, and its business school is named after him.) The point is every known Michiganian sphere of power was committed to the Harbaugh project. And the main thing Harbaugh had become known for at Stanford and San Francisco was overseeing a *power running game*. His preferred strategy was to run as much as possible, in a way that bordered on being condescending to the opponent.

The attentive reader may be able to guess where this is going, which is that while Harbaugh's Michigan teams were good at a number of things, they were mediocre when it came to running the football. In particular, they lost big games because they couldn't rush well enough to run out the clock when they were ahead. Michigan had the ball and a lead over Ohio State three times in the fourth quarter of their 2016 game but punted each time and ultimately lost. Throughout the 2018 season, broadcasters kept mentioning that the Michigan coaching staff wanted to use repeated power runs to throw "body blows" at the opposition, wearing out defenders through sheer force, in the hopes they would be too exhausted to hold up in the fourth quarter. Unfortunately, by the fourth quarter of Michigan's game against Ohio State in 2018, it was trailing by three touchdowns. It's hard to get a long-term body-blow strategy to work when your head gets punched off immediately.

Harbaugh's teams won ten games in 2015, 2016, and 2018, respectively, which is good, but he never beat Ohio State. In his fifth year, 2019, Michigan won nine games and lost to Ohio State. In his sixth year, it won two games and didn't play Ohio State because of COVID-19, but it probably would have lost. Harbaugh replaced the team's offensive coordinator in 2019, bringing in Josh Gattis, who was known to dabble in the spread-out, small-guys, modern stuff. Gattis's offense, however, still lost or nearly lost a number of games—most prominently the aforementioned 2020 Michigan State debacle—in which the team seemed stunned that it was unable to consistently run the ball down the middle of the field. Ohio State, over roughly this same period, had increasingly incorporated facets of the "spread" style, to the point that its offense was most successful when it threw short passes to smaller players. It had become, statistically, one of the best offenses in the history of the sport. Hilarious! Ha ha!

This—the idea of 2021 Michigan taking a breath, looking around, surveying the scene, thinking about the state of the world and its competition, and deciding that this was the year it was going to be able to run the ball down the middle of the field, pound the rock, and outphysical the opposition—is what needs to be understood about Thicc Stauskas's reaction to Sam Webb's report. It reminded one of the definition of insanity that is often misattributed, by alumni of lesser institutions, to Einstein: doing the same thing over and over again and expecting different results. Decent men and women may not have condoned the language Thicc Stauskas used, but they understood his frustration.

There had been a lot to get angry about over the course of the off-season, which in college football is an eight-month period during which nothing happens but does so very urgently. The meaning of the off-season's pseudo-events (staff changes, recruiting reports, practices that nobody in the press or public observes firsthand) are contested in a variety of forums; interpretations are cross-pollinated via message boards, blogs, Twitter accounts, group threads, and even sometimes personal interactions between humans. Michigan discussion nexuses include MGoBlog, the 247Sports message board, a different insider message board run by a company called Rivals, a third insider message board run by a company called On3 and founded by the same person who founded both Rivals and 247Sports, and more.

Usually, a college coach entering the last year of his contract either signs a contract extension or is terminated to avoid a lame-duck season, and the 2021 season was the last one covered by Harbaugh's original agreement with Michigan. But after the team's final 2020 game was canceled in early December, a month elapsed during which neither a termination nor a new contract was announced by athletic director Warde Manuel, a former Michigan defensive lineman whose patient air suggests a wisdom that has mostly been borne out in his decisions.

Author John U. Bacon, who lives in Ann Arbor and writes often about the football team, reported on December 7, 2020, that Manuel had discussed a new contract with Harbaugh and that the ball was in the coach's court. Sam Webb reported that Harbaugh was telling recruits he planned to sign an extension that would actually reduce his salary—the phrase he was using was "betting on himself." But the day on which these high school seniors could officially commit to playing at Michigan came and went in late December without this happening. There were some credible reports that Harbaugh was trying to find out if NFL teams were interested in hiring him. These reports were seized on by a splinter faction of fans who wanted to replace Harbaugh with Matt "Soup" Campbell of Iowa State, an Ohio native who had made the usually submediocre ISU Cyclones competitive. Someone changed the title of our Twitter group chat to "The Soup Group."

On January 8, 2021, however, Manuel and Harbaugh announced that a new five-year contract extension had been signed. The details were weird. Harbaugh would be taking a pay cut of 50 percent, from roughly $8 million a year to roughly $4 million, and his buyout—what he'd have to be paid by Michigan if he was fired—was likewise reduced from $10 million to $4 million. Four assistant coaches were let go, including the defensive coordinator. Manuel said in a statement that the football team "didn't achieve at a level that anyone expected this year."

Manuel's statement was a modest acknowledgement of reality, but retaining Harbaugh, even on a reduced salary, seemed to many to communicate a willingness to accept that level of achievement. The founder of MGoBlog—a tall, long-haired, and abundantly bearded computer engineering alumnus named Brian Cook, whose somewhat Viking-like appearance belies the stereotype of the physically withdrawn blogger—described himself as "baffled" by Harbaugh's continuing employment. Another fan site, Maize 'n' Brew, had already written that it was "time for the Jim Harbaugh era at Michigan to come to an end" and that "it is hard to think of any assistants that are proven or on the career upswing who would hitch their wagon to him." A columnist for the *Michigan Daily* student newspaper wrote that Harbaugh's monthlong delay in accepting the contract constituted the kind of "disrespect and disregard" for the university for which someone in his position could justifiably be fired.

The athletic department took the position that the COVID-19 year was an aberration and, aside from that, winning ten games (but not eleven, twelve, or thirteen, like a few other teams did) and occasionally beating other well-known programs (but not Ohio State) was not the worst status quo. It was attesting that Harbaugh was essentially a competent person who'd established a good foundation for recruiting and supervising football-playing students. Bacon, who, over the course of several Michigan-related books and a teaching appointment at the university, has become something like the ombudsman for the athletic program's ideals, noted on Twitter that the athletic department and university president were pleased that Harbaugh's players "have been very strong in the classroom and in the community."

It was true that team had won about two-thirds of its games with Harbaugh coaching, that its players had (according to NCAA-tracked graduation rate statistics) evidently been going to class and doing homework, and that both players and coaches had avoided committing or abetting crimes in the ways that have brought down many coaching regimes at other top football schools. But other facts suggested a terminal mediocrity spiral. The team was only 11-10 in its last twenty-one games. The margins of the losses were getting wider. Cutting a coach's salary in half could be read as an emasculating signal by recruits and potential assistant coaches, but even $4 million each year is quite an amount to pay someone just for seeing that roughly one hundred college students with extraordinary access to tutoring resources are staying on track to graduate and are not being arrested. Reader responses to the announcement of Harbaugh's reduced-salary extension on MGoBlog included words and phrases like "apathetic," "off the rails," "laughingstock," "worst deal any coach of a major program has ever signed," "none of this matters," "mediocrity personified," "failing marriage," and "weird, quirky, catatonic failure."

The university chose not to argue the point with its own ticket holders, students, or alumni, much less with the media. Neither Harbaugh nor Manuel conducted big-picture interviews with the press. (Manuel did appear on the athletic department's in-house podcast.) The team's spring scrimmage, which many other schools invite fans to watch for free, was closed to both fans and media coverage. (Ohio State opened both its scrimmage and one of the preceding practices to fans.) The program released a "highlight" video from the event that was sixty-eight seconds long and mostly shot in extreme close-up. The Michigan writers at 247Sports.com, a subscription service that depends on insider access and information and, thus, typically bends over backward not to attack the athletic department, called it "a pretty lame move," "a slap in the face," and "a brutal message" about the school's opinion of its own community. Brian Cook characterized the episode as "the program killing any goodwill that's left." Harbaugh and the athletic department, in public at least, were signaling a lack of urgency bordering on apathy. They seemed to care less than anyone else did, and it was driving people crazy.

There were some off-season developments that one could interpret as signs of a burgeoning renewal, but each seemed paired with another that supported the death-spiral theory. A new defensive secondary coach named Maurice Linguist arrived in January and exuded promising energy while securing several commitments from well-regarded high school players. He left the program three and a half months later to become the head coach of Buffalo, a State University of New York team that plays in the Mid-American Conference. A very talented wide receiver recruit named Xavier Worthy, who had graduated early from his high school, signed a letter of intent to play for Michigan despite the coaching situation, but then he asked to be released from his commitment so he could enroll at the University of Texas instead. Two former Michigan players who'd become up-and-coming coaches, Mike Hart and Ron Bellamy, accepted offers to join the staff, which suggested that the program, and Harbaugh, still had some currency. But four players who'd started games in 2020 transferred to other schools, which suggested Harbaugh may have "lost the locker room," a football coaching problem that is vaguely defined but always understood to be extremely bad. After one of the transfers, Thicc Stauskas wrote, "The only take I have to register about Michigan Football is that the vibes are fucked and the season is going to be a disaster."

When the sports reporting website The Athletic conducted an informal "Hope-O-Meter" survey in August 2021, Michigan fans finished as the sixtieth most hopeful out of the sixty-two teams whose fans responded. "I'm dead inside," one said. Season ticket purchases had dropped from ninety-two thousand in 2019 to eighty-four thousand in 2021. (There were no fans at the games in 2020 because of COVID-19.)

But here's the thing: everyone still cared. After all, eighty-four thousand season tickets is still a lot of season tickets! Traffic on the fan sites remained high. A lot of people said they had given up or didn't have any hopes for the season. But they were obviously lying, or they wouldn't have been talking about it so much.

Interlude

Jim Harbaugh, at Big Ten Media Day in August 2021, regarding the Nathan's Hot Dog Eating Contest and its perennial winner, Joey Chestnut:

I watch it every year. I'm a big fan. I don't miss that. Addie [Harbaugh's daughter] doesn't miss that. Sarah [his wife] likes it too. My son Jack loves it. There's no question about it [being impressive]. I mean, I've looked at some of his training, and he's just pretty awesome. Guy's the best at what he does; I have complete respect for that. He is an athlete, yeah. I mean if you are, if you were hot dog eating champion of the world, ate the most hot dogs in ten minutes in the world, would you consider that a sport? I think I would. I would probably feel pretty good about myself if I could do that.

On what food he could eat at Chestnut's level:

My mom always said I had a hollow leg. I'd probably say corn on the cob. I really like corn on the cob. I never tried [eating it competitively], but I'm always disappointed there's not another one to eat [in a regular dinner situation]. Usually, you got the pot there, and there's another one in there. There's one more? I'll eat that one too. I'm disappointed there's not a couple more.

CHAPTER

4

WESTERN MICHIGAN

COLLEGE FOOTBALL IS in some sense Thomas Jefferson's fault.
Higher education in what would become the United States initially revolved around schools like Harvard and Princeton, which
at the time provided religious and "classical" (Latin, Greek, etc.)
educations to future members of the clergy and others in the social
upper class. Jefferson had a lot of thoughts about this, as he did
about every other subject, and he believed that such a limited
scope of education was inadequate to the kind of country he
wanted the United States to become, in which every citizen (if
they were a white man) would be equipped by institutions of
learning, equal in stature to those in Europe, to handle their own
farm or business and to participate in the public discourse of
democracy.

With this end goal in mind, his vision for American education
was one in which everyone "from the highest to the poorest"

would receive public schooling to some degree, with the most promising (among white men) passed on to higher levels regardless of their original social status. Even at the most advanced levels, Jefferson wanted curricula to cover subjects of practical use, like chemistry, agriculture, and the activities that would soon thereafter be referred to as engineering. He agitated constantly to create a federal flagship university and associated schooling system; he didn't succeed in this even as president, but he did found the University of Virginia, which became a model for the many (relatively) egalitarian state universities across the country that aspired to create graduates who were both economically productive and well-read. He was also one of the main influences on the Land Ordinance of 1785 and the Northwest Territorial Ordinance of 1787, which allotted land that potential new states were required to sell or lease in order to fund public education. Sixty years later, the Morrill Land-Grant College Act of 1862 would give away more land (which, to be clear, was in federal possession only because it'd been taken from the Native Americans who'd been living on it for thousands of years) for the purpose of starting even more colleges. That bill's sponsor, Vermont representative Justin Smith Morrill, echoed Jefferson in saying that he hoped the institutions to be launched would be "accessible to all, but especially to the sons of toil."

The University of Michigan, in fact, was cofounded by a man named Augustus Woodward, who had been appointed by Jefferson in 1805 to be the Michigan Territory's chief justice. With the self-confidence typical of guys and dudes of that era, Woodward decided that the university should be organized around thirteen categories of knowledge that he had defined and named himself. Michigan never used Woodward's system, however, because while it was technically founded in 1817 as a Detroit institution, it didn't have the resources to actually teach any students until 1841, at which point it was located in Ann Arbor because that was where some local white landowners had some land. (The United States bought the southwest corner of the state from several Native American tribes in 1807 for $10,000 and an agreement to make $2,400 in annual payments going forward.) According to Howard Peckham's 1967 book *The Making of the University of Michigan*, President James Monroe later decided not to reappoint Woodward to the judgeship after the members of the Detroit bar complained in writing about "his entire want of practical knowledge." Monroe gave Woodward a job in Florida instead, in an early foreshadowing of the type of guys who would end up populating Florida.

The University of Michigan's story from there is one of essentially continuous expansion along the lines Jefferson would have advocated. In 1855, U of M added a science curriculum; in 1865, it surpassed Harvard to briefly become the largest university in the country by enrollment. It was led by a series of presidents who enacted what were, for their time, progressive policies, such as making chapel services optional and letting students select specific classes and areas of study. (Most notable among these presidents was James Angell, who negotiated the installation in his official residence of Ann Arbor's first indoor toilet as a condition of taking the job.) In the early twentieth century, the university became a destination for Jewish students on the East Coast who had been excluded from Ivy League schools by anti-Semitic quotas.

Michigan was concurrently prospering as a state. It was initially covered in white pine trees, which were in demand for construction in part because they were very tall and had few branches below the canopy level, which made for a desirable ratio of smooth to knotted wood. Per the Bureau of Labor Statistics, Michigan was the top lumber producer in the country during each of the first three censuses taken after the Civil War. As that industry declined because there were no more white pines to harvest, some of the fortunes it had created were invested in the burgeoning automotive sector, which subsequently did pretty well as far as making a vast amount of money and completely changing the nature of day-to-day existence. Detroit's population grew from roughly 285,000 in 1900 to 1.8 million by 1950, and Michigan's per capita income in 1955 was 16 percent higher than the US average.

U of M accrued a truly impressive account of relevance, most of it good. It opened the first university-owned hospital; an early medical graduate, William James Mayo, went on to work with his brother in the practice that became the Mayo Clinic. Clarence Darrow attended the law school for a year before dropping out to finish his preparation for the bar privately. Philosopher John Dewey was a professor in the 1880s; Robert Frost was a visiting teacher in the 1920s. Leo Burnett, the founder of modern advertising, overlapped on campus with Branch Rickey, who would go on to sign Jackie Robinson to the Dodgers; Arthur Miller overlapped with Gerald Ford. Mike Wallace, Gilda Radner, and Bob McGrath (from *Sesame Street*) were alums, while Iggy Pop (who in 1995, well after becoming a rock icon, manifested the well-rounded Michigan ideal by writing a short review of *The Decline and Fall of the Roman Empire* for a classics journal) and Madonna dropped out. The announcement that Jonas Salk's polio vaccine was effective took place in Ann Arbor—Salk had previously worked at the school of public health—as did John F. Kennedy's introduction of the Peace Corps and Lyndon Johnson's introduction of the Great Society (i.e., Medicare and Medicaid). The Students for a Democratic Society's Port Huron statement, the defining '60s declaration of leftist principles, was written while SDS leader Tom Hayden was a student (Port Huron is one hundred miles away). The militant Weather Underground group and the weather app Weather Underground both have U of M roots, the latter as a nod to the former, which is actually kind of weird. Jack "Dr. Death" Kevorkian was a 1952 med-school graduate. And needless to say, we must not forget the Unabomber (MA '64, PhD '67).

The school's place in the American imagination perhaps reached its apex in the 1983 movie *The Big Chill*, which was co-written and directed by Lawrence Kasdan, an alum who had just come off writing *Raiders of the Lost Ark* and the original *Star Wars* sequels. The characters in *The Big Chill* are semidisillusioned friends reuniting for a funeral fifteen years after graduating from college; in the film, their biographies and arcs are constructed so as to encompass the breadth of (white) baby boomer experience. The school that these representatives of the zeitgeist attended together is Michigan. At one point, they watch a Michigan–Michigan State football game on TV and, in a true-to-life depiction, complain bitterly about the team. Jeff Goldblum's character says they always "fold in the fourth quarter."

Ah, yes—Michigan, like other state universities, also had football. (In real life, the program beat Michigan State in the game whose footage was used for the movie and went on to win the Rose Bowl that season. Suck on that, Jeff Goldblum!) The connection between college and football now strikes many people as arbitrary, but when viewed historically, it may have been inevitable. The higher education system Jefferson helped create was a novel one by the standards of the rest of the world; rather than being controlled by a central government or church, each state's system competed with every other's for students and had to find its own funding. (The states and territories in which they were located were themselves competing for residents and investment money.) America's ivory towers, whose occupants are often imagined to exist apart from the pressures and tawdry incentives of normal life, are actually engaged in constant competition for popularity, wealth, and prestige.

For this reason, Professor J. Douglas Toma explained in a 2003 book called *Football U*, colleges wanted members of the local population, even if they weren't alumni, to feel like part of their community because it meant their children might end up as paying students and their representatives in state legislatures might be more generous with budget assistance. Local business owners and other civic leaders likewise benefited from universities that became regional and national beacons. As Paul Putz, a Baylor University historian (and Nebraska native and University of Nebraska football fan), told me, "That sense of competition between states is also related to the autonomy and independence that states would claim for themselves in places like Virginia or Michigan." He went on, "It's not just symbolic, but it is very much about power and control of resources, tied in with the competition for new residents. So if you're wanting to attract people to your state and then get them to move there, a university or a college could be important."

At the time when many of the United States' colleges were founded, domestic travel and relocation were time-consuming and expensive, which meant both that state identity was more important vis-à-vis national identity than it is today and that being able to train professionals locally was a practical necessity. Said Putz,

> If we think about region and place in the nineteenth-century world, there's far more isolation than today. They're constructing railroads, but the transcontinental railroad isn't in place until after the Civil War. New technologies like the telegraph are emerging, but it still takes a long time to move from place to place. So there's much more rootedness. Of course there is migration, but people are often moving from one isolated community to another. Distance matters. And so it becomes more important for states to have an institution of higher education where they can train their people. This is connected to the nation, this is connected to a sense of American identity, but it also is connected to a sense of place and purpose for a particular territory.

The game of American football—which evolved from rugby in the second half of the nineteenth century via rules adjustments made by, among others, Yale's Walter Camp—fit into this array of circumstances perfectly. It appealed to college-aged men, it attracted local interest and built local pride, and it rewarded strength, strategic intellect, and organizational efficiency. The game first caught on in the Ivy League; as Putz explained, this East Coast version of the game had pretensions to the aristocratic English ideal of amateurism, in which sports were kept separate from business so as not to corrupt the spirit of competition and self-betterment for its own sake. But as college football began attracting paying customers, educational leaders expressed alarm. How could they maintain an amateur ideal when business was clearly booming?

This concern—and, one might argue, the reality that its member schools already had more money and prestige than anyone else and did not need their sports teams to build more of it—would eventually lead the Ivy League schools to abandon big-time football in favor of a more modest approach. The Midwest's spin on the idea, however, was that you could do big business and still have ideals—that it was actually good for ostensibly "amateur" scholars to play a violent game within a commercial milieu because it prepared them to dominate the rest of their lives in the same way. The sport allowed colleges to attract attention while fulfilling a core social mission—preparing the most promising children from farm communities to manage smelting facilities and so forth—as well. Many of Michigan's collections are digitized; when you search them for the word *football*, papers and photographs come up that were collected by student enthusiasts of the sport who went on to become distinguished alums in robust, manly Manifest Destiny fields like lumber, automobiles, and shipping.

The unofficial spokesman for the Midwestern football ideal was Amos Alonzo Stagg, who coached at the University of Chicago—at the time, a Big Ten powerhouse. Said Putz, "In 1931,

Stagg is interviewed, and he's asked about the excesses of sports. They ask him if this whole overemphasis on winning and the attention we give to college sports, isn't this corrupting young people? Isn't it 'low and unworthy'? And he responds, 'Low and unworthy! Low and unworthy, to want to win? Golly, man, isn't that what life's all about?'"

————◆————

Michigan's contribution to this ethos is documented in an athletic archives collection created thirty years ago. (Michigan was, appropriately, the first place to have a scholarly collection of football documents.) The collection is housed at the Bentley Historical Library, which is located in the university's quiet, leafy North Campus area inside a low-slung, 1970s brick building down the street from Gerald Ford's presidential archive.

The library is lined with red carpet, and its large plate-glass windows look out on a garden. In a conference room, I got a briefing on school football history from archivist Greg Kinney, a soft-spoken man who has white hair and a white mustache. The central figure in early Michigan football, he explained, was Charles Baird, a sort of fan-coach-manager-hustler—he never actually played for the team—from the class of 1895. Michigan's squad was created in 1879, a decade after Princeton and Rutgers played the first intercollegiate game (Rutgers won, and I believe that may have been the program's last victory). Baird was the one who got the sport off the ground as a fixture of campus life; John U. Bacon credits him with essentially inventing the concept of the athletic director and pioneering a formally school-affiliated athletic department funded by charging admission to games. Kinney notes that Baird organized what he called "alumni games," which Michigan identifies as being the first homecoming games, although several other universities also claim they invented homecoming.

Kinney showed me a box of Baird's correspondence, and aside from the formality (even brief, mundane exchanges were made in longhand on letterhead), there was little in the collection that would have felt out of place to any follower of the modern sports scene. There was a letter to Baird from an armchair quarterback at Williams College explaining how to beat Cornell: "I tell you Charlie, you want to send your interference farther out around the ends on end plays." There was a letter from 1897, on which Baird had been copied, in which an assistant coach implored a player named James T. Hogg to serve as captain because of the effect it would have on intangibles. "There isn't another Michigan player who could inspire the confidence and determination in a team that you can," the letter's author wrote. There was a letter to Baird from a Lafayette College student named E. Gard Edwards, who was considering an offer to play "end or half-back" while attending U of M medical school and felt that the program ought to know that having a bit more money in his pocket would go a long way toward making that decision easier. "Finances are of considerable moment to me," Edwards wrote, clarifying that while he did not "believe in professionalism" (of course not, E. Gard!) or "expect to be paid for services," he nonetheless felt it relevant to note that the University of Pennsylvania had offered to cover his room and board and that "if I go to U. of M. I should like to have the same concession and a scholarship." (Added Edwards, "You can rest assured that all correspondence on this matter is sacredly confidential as far as I am concerned." He may not have gotten what he wanted from either Penn or Michigan, because records show that in the following season, he became head football coach at Washington & Jefferson College, near Pittsburgh.)

At Michigan, football was another way to keep up the university's profile relative to the East Coast icons of higher education. Coach-turned-athletic-director Fielding Yost designed and built Michigan Stadium in 1927 in response to the venues that had been erected at rivals Minnesota and Ohio State. Yost put together a scrapbook of images to inspire himself, Kinney said, which included both the Roman Colosseum (modesty!) and the Yale Bowl. He marketed the bonds that financed Michigan Stadium's construction to the general public, offering seats between the forty-yard lines in exchange for bond purchases. His catchphrase was, "Athletics for all." Said Kinney, "He genuinely believed that, but it was also a very convenient way to get money for the athletic department." At Michigan and elsewhere, the oft-remarked-upon category of people who didn't attend a college but developed an attachment to its teams—fans of other schools call them "Walmart Wolverines" because of where they are assumed to have gotten their team gear—was created intentionally.

Yost's most significant successor in the field of cash accumulation was Don Canham, a track coach who was hired as athletic director in 1968. Canham sold season tickets via direct mail with what were, for the time, flashy, four-color brochures promoting the purchase, as Bacon has written, in less-than-subtle fashion to women as a way to get their husbands and children out of the house for an entire Saturday. Canham hired Bo Schembechler and launched Michigan into the era in which every sports facility (and even some coaching staff titles, like the "Sanford Robertson Offensive Coordinator" position) is named after donors, setting it up with systemic resources that seem almost insurmountable to most other schools. (They aren't always insurmountable! Just ask Appalachian State! And then set me on fire and throw me out of a helicopter!)

Michigan's fight song, "The Victors," written in 1889, emphasizes that its players are "Champions of the West," as in the Western Conference, the predecessor of the Big Ten, so named when states like Michigan and Ohio were not too long removed from being considered the country's western frontier. I found a reference to Michigan as "the Harvard of the West" in a magazine from 1909, and to Harvard as "the Michigan of the East" (you can get T-shirts that say this) in an alumni publication from 1937. (And also, very randomly, in an ahead-of-the-curve University of Oklahoma periodical from 1936.) A 1948 football yearbook describes U of M's athletic facilities as "working monuments to the Michigan ideal of education for a well-rounded life" and mentions that its current football staff "maintains the same degree of balance and scholarship that has always distinguished Michigan." A contemporaneous book called *Modern Football*, written by long-time Michigan coach Fritz Crisler, recommends "hardening" one's muscles during preseason training with activities that include "rolling on the floor" and "diving on the ground." Thus rose the Michigan Man, judiciously balancing his scholarship and civic leadership with muscles hardened from smashing his face into the ground on purpose.

———◆———

It was not the salad days for the United States, the state of Michigan, or its flagship university's men when I arrived in Ann Arbor for the opening football game of the 2021 season. For one, the school had recently issued a report, compiled by an outside law firm, about more than one thousand instances of sexual abuse allegedly committed between 1966 and 2003 by a university doctor named Robert Anderson during physical examinations of athletes and other students. The report documented evidence that university authority figures, including Bo Schembechler and Don Canham, failed to act on students' contemporary accounts of feeling uncomfortable (or worse) about Anderson's exams. The report cited four accounts given by athletes who said they told Schembechler they believed Anderson had done something improper, and Canham is alleged to have been told at least twice about potential misconduct while the doctor was affiliated with the athletic department; neither of the men is known to have pursued an investigation of the allegations. (The university announced a settlement of just under $500 million with 1,050 accusers in related litigation in January 2022. Anderson died in 2008.)

In the local history section of a bookstore called Nicola's, located in a tasteful strip mall on the west side of town, the titles told a story of decline. Among them were *Forgotten Landmarks of Detroit*, *A $500 House in Detroit*, *Fading Ads of Detroit*, *Teardown*, and *The Poisoned City* (the latter two about Flint). There is a book called *Detroit City Is the Place to Be* by a writer named Mark Binelli, but its title (taken from a Ted Nugent song) is wistful— Binelli writes about moving back to the city at a time when it was, to most people, not the place to be at all. Foreign competition started threatening the Big Three automakers in the 1960s, and the companies began to move their manufacturing abroad. The decline of this sector, when combined with the rise of segregated suburbs, was devastating to the Black populations of cities like Detroit, Flint, and Saginaw.

At the time of the game, a third wave of COVID-19 was spreading through the population, with more than two thousand new cases being reported in the state each day, one of the highest rates in the nation. Employment and consumption shocks had left many local businesses either partially or fully closed because of cash-flow problems and understaffing. When I parked downtown on Thursday, the sun's long late-afternoon rays were falling on mostly empty stretches of sidewalk. The café at which I intended to buy an iced coffee was closed, the next one I found was closed as well, and I ended up drinking a hot coffee poured over ice by a nonplussed bartender at the Jolly Pumpkin brewpub. Entire sections of wrought-iron outdoor tables were empty because there was no one to wait on them. Long strings of the concession stands under the bleachers would be shuttered at the game itself.

Many citizens had nevertheless chosen to not be vaccinated against the disease that was responsible for all of this, which spoke to a wider distrust in expertise and institutions that had been made absurdly explicit months earlier when federal authorities accused a number of local "militia" members of planning to kidnap and possibly murder Democratic governor Gretchen Whitmer because of mask rules and other pandemic-related restrictions she had imposed. Michigan had come a long way in the wrong direction from Jonas Salk, it seemed. (As of this writing, two of the men have been acquitted, two pleaded guilty, and others are still facing charges.)

On the other end of the political spectrum, the leftist political movement of "democratic socialists" had popularized a critique of elite "meritocratic" entities like U of M, which were accused of helping entrench the upper class at the same time they condemned students who weren't already rich to a lifetime of student debt in the stagnant middle and lower income brackets. Across the street from my parking spot downtown, there was a new high-rise luxury building—one of several that are widely perceived as being targeted to wealthy out-of-state students—called the Varsity. Rent for its 430-square-foot studio apartments started at $2,169 per month.

Black Lives Matter activism, in which a number of Michigan football players had participated, had moreover drawn attention to racial segregation in ostensibly progressive cities and institutions like Ann Arbor and U of M, whose Black populations (7 percent for the city, 4 percent for the school) are significantly lower than the Black population in the state, which is 15 percent. (The university has, it's worth noting, been held back in efforts to maintain a diverse student body by a 2006 state law that forbids it from considering race in admissions. In the 1990s, Black enrollment was as high as 8.9 percent.)

It was a fraught time to be a tradition-obsessed institution that purported to value merit, rule following, and success, and that was in the back of some fans' minds when they argued about Harbaugh.

One was university regent Jordan Acker, a gregarious, high-energy thirty-six-year-old who, like the other seven regents who hold ultimate power over the school by virtue of being able to hire and fire its presidents and approve its budget, won his position in a statewide election. Acker, who is a lawyer, a Democrat, and a major U of M sports fan, said,

> I always tell people that the same problems that Democrats have in Ohio are the same problems Michigan has in Ohio. What we've seen in Ohio over the last thirty to forty years, maybe longer even, is a demographic shift. The belt from Akron through Youngstown, or from Youngstown to Akron into Cleveland to Toledo, was an area at the University of Michigan that was our prime recruiting territory for decades. And not only that, the people in that area, there are Michigan fans pretty much everywhere, to the point where Toledo's like a fifty-fifty town. The problem has been that a lot of people left northern Ohio as the population has shifted south and west. And as Columbus has grown, and Cincinnati, and those suburbs have grown, you see less and less people who are Michigan fans. Those big high schools in southern Ohio and central Ohio don't send kids to U of M. It's made recruiting in Ohio a lot more difficult, because these kids, now they are raised in areas that are 100 percent Buckeye areas.

His theory checks out. Desmond Howard and Charles Woodson, among many other Wolverine standouts, were from northern Ohio, and its Democratic-leaning working-class population has been shrinking in proportion to more Republican parts of Ohio for years. (Northern Ohio's white population, for the record, has also become less Democratic, especially since Donald Trump's 2016 campaign.)

Acker raised the issue within the context of the so-called name, image, and likeness (NIL) legislation that had been passed by states across the country. The bills called for college athletes to be able to be paid for product endorsements and the like without losing their NCAA eligibility. Shortly before the season started, the NCAA had abandoned its opposition to such payments. Acker was diplomatically critical of the conservatism with which the university administration had handled the issue in preceding years, feeling that it should have been a leader in advocating affirmatively for such rights. In addition to being a less offensively unfair way to divide some of the vast revenue generated by major sports, Acker said, NIL was the sort of thing that was practically incumbent upon a program with high academic standards to explore as a means of, well, winning more without having to abandon its standards.

"Michigan fans want to win and want players to graduate, and they want lots of wins and lots of players graduating. And they're not willing to sacrifice one for the other, they're just not," he said. He was effusive in praising Harbaugh and Manuel for their attention to the scholar-athlete ideal. But he also admitted the scholar-athlete ideal had not quite been getting it done recently in late November. "It's not a sustainable path—I can't ask Michigan fans to accept losing to OSU. I wouldn't want them to. But we have to take advantage of everything we can to make that happen, obviously, within our values as an institution."

It was, frankly, a tough spot.

———◆———

On the other hand, there was a goddang football game to be played. "We enjoy our lives because that's what God wants," the late Jack Gilbert argues in a poem called "A Brief for the Defense," which is about the classic question of how all-encompassing our

despair should be amid the world's inexhaustible supply of suffer-
ing, sickness, starvation, sorrow, "awfulness," and "slaughter." If
we were not also meant to experience happiness despite these burdens, he asserts, "the mornings before summer dawn would not be
made so fine" and "the Bengal tiger would not be fashioned so
miraculously well." September weekends in the football territories of the upper Midwest were also made fine: the crowds hum-
ming with energy, the helmets polished, the sky an endless blue.

Much of southeast and central Michigan is flat and has been
cleared for farmland or divided into "charter townships," which
are quasi-municipal, Michigan-specific zoning designations whose
legal meaning I'm too bored to look up even for the purposes of
finishing this sentence, but which seem to mostly encompass sub-
divisions serviced by strip-mall, big-box, and franchise-restaurant
complexes of varying sizes. They can feel interchangeable. Ann
Arbor, by contrast, is in a pocket of hills. Its borders enclose a cultural cornucopia of non–chain restaurants, bars that run the
gamut from classy to disgusting (there is one called the Eight Ball,
which is a euphemism for a bag of cocaine, and it smells like pee,
or at least it used to; my apologies to the Eight Ball if it got rid of
the pee smell), musical venues of various sizes, expensive coffee
shops, gourmet grocery stores, and two theaters with old-time
marquee signs. College towns are where American states and
regions that for the most part do not prioritize soulfulness or distinctiveness keep a reserve of soul and distinctiveness, and Ann
Arbor is the preeminent example of that, unless you count Madison, which I don't, because I haven't been there.

For all its big-budget aspects, college football is still for the
most part played in these smaller towns and cities that are otherwise not set up to handle crowds. While newer pro stadiums and
arenas are generally located at the center of parking lot complexes,
dedicated freeway exits, and other support amenities, college football games are like asteroids landing on areas that, for the other

358-odd days a year, are just regular places. Michigan Stadium is bordered by a golf course, a high school, and a rental-heavy residential neighborhood. (Older pro stadiums such as Fenway Park, Wrigley Field, and Lambeau Field—affiliated, perhaps not coincidentally, with some of the most valuable and beloved franchises—are located in these kinds of settings too.) It's a single-deck bowl built into a hill, supported by blocks-long walls of red brick several stories high and flanked at each end by two gigantic blue signs, visible from far yonder, that say "M." It's past the south end of the academic campus, a fifteen-minute walk from the main quad area and downtown, such that game day creates a ceremonial mass migration of the city's population. It is the biggest stadium in North America, which is awesome.

In the little plaza by the gates, a guy who's become famous online for wearing an unnerving full-body wolverine costume with strange blue eyes, known colloquially as the Murderwolf, was hanging around giving high-fives. The bleachers were not quite packed, but there were no empty sections. Recent history weighed on the mood, but Harbaugh had brought in a number of young, energetic coaches, and (as always) there were a lot of players on the roster who seemed like they had serious potential. If they all got going in the same direction, without any of the bouts of teamwide malaise and confusion that had marred recent history, maybe they would win some games.

I was sitting at about the ten-yard line some seventy rows up with a guy named Alex, a tall, young gentleman with dark hair who was part of the Twitter group direct-message conversation. He had an ambivalence about Michigan and life in general that I related to—it was sometimes so strong that it seemed reflected in his posture—and he had actually invited me into the chat, which aside from me is mostly alums or Michigan natives in their late twenties. They are all leftists of varying degrees, and they are deeply emotionally invested in college football outcomes despite their awareness that the sport is exploitative and dangerous. They are (I think justifiably) grouchy about the financial situation that baby boomers have put their generation in, and they believe there should be much more federal social spending that might benefit them, although they must have at least some amount of disposable income available because they are always exchanging information about the state of their sports gambling. (They're all great guys, and despite often buying IPAs that cost $3.99 per can, I also believe there should be more social spending, and that it should benefit my family.)

The public address announcer opened proceedings by alluding to the strange circumstances in which the 2020 season had been (partly) played. "After 644 days away," he said, "good morning and welcome to Michigan Stadium." The band's drum major successfully leaned back, limbo-style, and touched his big fuzzy hat to the ground, as per tradition. There was an A-10 Warthog flyover and a paratrooper landing, which was narrated from the field by a guy with a microphone who was wearing the kind of busy skulls-and-flowers shirt that energy-drink MMA enthusiasts wear. "Sleepy Joe [Biden] is revitalizing the flyover industry," Alex said to me, cryptically and leftistly. (I have since discussed the remark with him; he claims its meaning is evident.)

There was a big cheer when James Earl Jones's face appeared on the video board playing the team's pregame hype video, which he narrates using a script that was written in part by Harbaugh. (Jones is an alumnus from the class of 1955.) It begins with Jones very dramatically picking up a pair of headphones in a recording booth—and is, I think it can be safely said, the only football hype video that brags that the team's fans "respect integrity and honor excellence." ("We are the greatest university in the world," he adds, and when he says it, it sounds true, even though the greatest university in the world is known to be Harvard, which is the school I actually attended, because of my excellence.) I felt a modest release of dopamine in my brain when the board cut to a live shot of Harbaugh waddling between the team and the wall of the tunnel where it was waiting to take the field. (His gait bears the jutting wonkiness of fourteen eventful years in the NFL.) That was still my guy. Our guy. Maybe.

The atmosphere early in the game was apprehensive. Western was a decent team, but Michigan should beat decent teams, and a loss on this Saturday would have pointed strongly toward things being really bad again this year. After all the mental work everyone had done following the previous season to get themselves ready to at least consider the possibility of a winning season, a loss would have really let the air out.

Looking back, I think the whole situation turned on a third down completion to a tight end named Erick All on the team's first possession of the year. Michigan had struggled on third downs the previous season, as well as on the other downs. Despite All being an obviously superior athlete and a smiley, well-liked person around the program, he had had a bad season individually, flat-out dropping four well-thrown, easy passes in memorable situations.

On the first series of its first drive, facing a third and three from its own thirty-two-yard line, the play Michigan ran called for All to run a slant, which is what it sounds like. On the recording of the game, quarterback Cade McNamara appears to look at All before any other receiver. If the pass had been wide, or if God forbid All had dropped it, there surely would have been grumbling, murmuring, and perhaps even groaning. Stomachs on and off the field would have begun to clench. Who knows how things would have gone in the rest of the game and beyond? Analytics experts sometimes argue that phenomena like "clutchness" and "choking" aren't real, or at least aren't statistically observable, but every fan knows when their team is or isn't borking it out there.

Without hesitating, though, McNamara threw a perfect pass that All caught in stride for a decisive first down. Eight plays later,

Michigan scored. Miles beneath our feet, the earth had begun to move.

The crowd roared loudest when micro-bodybuilder and running back Blake Corum, who looks and plays like a cannonball, broke into the secondary with only one safety to beat for a touchdown. *Good luck to that guy*, I thought, and Corum flew around and past him for the score. But the next loudest cheer was for the extra offensive linemen who ran on to help gain a first down on a fourth and short in a pile of pushing and grunting over which Hassan Haskins, a "mooseback" in MGoBlog terminology, and one of especially indomitable will, carried the ball. Say what you want about modernizing an offense. No one can resist the ancestral call of the jumbo package when it's doing its job.

The biggest star of the first half for Michigan was wide receiver Ronnie Bell. On my drive to Ann Arbor, I had listened to Bell's appearance on a podcast hosted by Michigan's self-deprecating third- and fourth-string quarterbacks. In a Missouri drawl, Bell told them he can jump thirty-eight or forty inches high, depending on whether he takes a step first, and mentioned having been able to score nearly every time he had the ball on his high school basketball team. (Newspaper articles and highlight clips confirm his claims.) To put things in context, this was the profile of a recruit who wasn't considered to have "elite athleticism," and who wasn't offered a scholarship by schools besides Michigan to play football, because he was skinny and wasn't, relatively speaking, that fast. At the highest levels of the college game, you can have a forty-inch vertical and enough hand-eye coordination to routinely score thirty points in competitive basketball and still be considered a longshot and a grinder.

Bell even initially committed to a Missouri college to play basketball. Then, he said, he admitted to his father that he'd rather try to play football instead. (In the latter sport, he was the Kansas City area's player of the year.) His dad told him to trust his instincts, and he went to Michigan. There, he earned a reputation as a team leader who practiced and played with constant energy. During games, he ran with a spindly grace around and past more highly rated recruits in opposing secondaries. Heading into the 2021 season, his senior year, he was voted as a captain by his teammates and was expected to be the team's best wideout.

That expectation was fulfilled almost immediately: in the second quarter, Bell broke open on a bomb downfield with a tidy out-and-in fake, caught the pass, and scored a seventy-six-yard touchdown. Before that, he'd caught a long pass with one hand near the sideline only to be dubiously flagged for offensive pass interference. The next time he touched the ball was on a punt return, which he ran thirty-one yards before being grabbed by the leg and barely taken down.

When Bell tried to get up, he couldn't put weight on the leg that had been grabbed. In the crowd, there was hopeful speculation that it had cramped up in the late summer weather. That optimism dissipated in my section, which was behind the team's bench, when a team staffer wearing a white polo shirt climbed into the stands and summoned an older man in a customized Bell jersey to return with him to the sideline. It was Ronnie's father, Aaron, being taken to see his son. The younger Bell was soon seated, with his legs out straight and a towel covering his face, on the modified golf cart used to transport injured players on the slow ride down the sideline and around the end zone to the locker room. He had suffered a torn ACL and would not play again in 2021. If there's one way that football definitely reflects the rest of life, it's that it is cruel and arbitrary.

By early in the second half, Michigan was leading 33-7. They were dominating a lesser team, but there were reasons to think they could keep it up against better competition. The offense was judiciously distributing the ball around the field to its various fast, talented players, which it had been claiming it was going to start doing for years. It was, indeed, also running up the middle, and successfully so. The players in the defensive secondary seemed to have a collective idea who was going to guard which guy from the other team on any given play, a huge improvement over the previous year.

During the fourth quarter, Alex and I discussed the university, national politics, and the future. He had closely followed the contentious 2016 Democratic primary between Bernie Sanders and Hillary Clinton during his time in school. On the one hand, Sanders's campaign, among other things, had made him uneasy about the role that institutions like Michigan play in passing on economic advantages from generation to generation. (He is from a family of five Michigan alumni, two parents and three kids.) On the other hand, it was not as if a degree from the university still guaranteed access to a network of hiring directors offering secure middle-class employment, if it ever had. His job at the time was writing web copy designed to capture Google search traffic for a large company. (On the side, he wrote a blog, *Grandvillain*, about the enormous apartment complex, which was designed and constructed to look like a Bavarian castle, but in a remarkably half-assed way, where he lived in the West Michigan city of Grandville.)

It was fine, though. "Liberal arts degrees are maybe not the best for getting you a ton of money so you can buy a boat, but I do think that I got a great education," he said. He was proud of himself and his siblings for meeting the school's admissions standards and doing the work to graduate, and he had been disappointed that COVID-19 had meant 2020 was the first year in his memory he had not gone to Ann Arbor in the fall. "I've found a really great sense of community here for basically my entire life," he said.

He was one of the more pessimistic members of the chat regarding the team's chances, pointing out correctly that the common link between the team's Harbaugh-era offenses, which had been led by varying coordinators and employed varying styles but still ranged only from okay to mediocre, was the head coach, who was supposed to be an expert on offense. With that said, he had already made plans to go to three more Michigan games in person during the season. We are who we are!

———◆———

The final score was 47-14. I attended the postgame press conference, which given all the money Michigan and other top college football schools spend on their facilities, was surprisingly held in a conference-room space in the basketball arena adjacent to the stadium. It was funny to see an actual press conference after having seen so many dramatic clips of coaches barking at reporters and sweating tough questions. Typical postgame pressers, it turns out, are casual and boring. To emphasize this, the writer seated front and center was wearing a polo shirt with the color and radiative properties of nuclear waste. One of Harbaugh's kids (he has seven; this one appeared to be eleven or twelve years old) was waiting to hug him when he walked in, which was an interesting reminder that he is a real, tangible human person and not just a symbol for people to argue about on TV and Twitter. (One of his children was born in 2011, when he was coaching the 49ers. He told reporters his wife, Sarah, had done a "great job.")

There were not a lot of smiles and small talk in the room. This was understandable. The premise of the situation was that there was to be an interaction between the coach and the press, and most of these members of the press had probably written or said at some point in the preceding year that this coach was going to be, or should have been, subject to a justified termination. Moreover, when Harbaugh's team loses, as it had done in most of its games the previous year, he performs a ritual of being terse, to the point of clipping out pronouns and articles from his sentences ("Team is gonna own this." "Played hard. Gotta strengthen the resolve"), as if to show that he doesn't have the time to bother with the less

necessary words when there is so much football work to do. The
press doesn't like this. So there we all were, vague enemies, kind of
talking.

That notwithstanding, Harbaugh took the time to explain
some of the game's strategic storylines with moderate looseness.
"We were stopping the run, and played more coverages, which
made the quarterback hold the ball a *liiittle* bit longer, and we
were able to apply some pressure," he said in summarizing the
second half. This was a small gift to the press. A leading theory
about one of the new coaches, defensive coordinator Mike Mac-
Donald, was that he had been brought in to "diversify" the team's
defensive pass-coverage schemes. Here, the head coach was sort of
confirming that theory. ("We needed some changeups, and we
needed to show some different looks. We needed to disguise some
coverages," Harbaugh added later.) A détente was being offered.

I was sitting next to a sportswriter I'd met the previous day
and noticed he had Twitter open. Cell reception is dodgy in the
stands, so I hadn't been following the reaction to the game online.
I asked him what the word was among internet people about this
thirty-three-point win. "They're complaining that he [Harbaugh]
let Ronnie Bell return a punt," he said. There was still some distance to go for Jim, as far as earning back the trust of the rabble.
Onward to next week and a nationally televised night game
against the University of Washington.

During the game, a fortysomething man and his daughter had
sat behind Alex and me. The man lived in Marion, Indiana (about
three hours south) and said he was a fan of Michigan because his
parents were both from the city of Inkster, a historically working-
class community outside Detroit. He was in the area visiting family over Labor Day. It became organically clear that his vibes were
in alignment with Alex's and mine, as far as knowing the name
of every player who took the field, even the backups. He urged
them on individually under his breath and got excited when

they did something good, even if it was quite minor, and he exhaled in disappointment when they did something wrong, but in a patient way. We had, of course, never met before. But at one point during the first quarter, when the score was still close and things still seemed touch-and-go, he briefly put both hands on my shoulders after an adverse play, a quick gesture of reassurance between friends.

Interlude

Jim Harbaugh, in September 2021, forty years after the last episode of The Rockford Files, *upon being asked about the Apple TV sitcom* Ted Lasso:

It's absolutely the best show on TV. It's right up there with, I'd put it up there with *The Rockford Files*. It's that good.

CHAPTER

5

WASHINGTON

THE FOLLOWING COMMENTS, with the exception of one that is labeled as such, were made by users on MGoBlog.com and 247Sports.com's Michigan Insider site before, during, and after Michigan's September 11, 2021, night game against the University of Washington at Michigan Stadium. Michigan won the game 31-10 and was not tied with, or losing to, the Huskies at any point after the first score of the game. They're in chronological order; all times are in EDT.

UM_Ftown, 8:09 p.m.
Ready to be disappointed.

rob6reid, 8:23 p.m.
Why the fuck is the crowd making so much noise

R.J. MacReady, 8:25 p.m.
Those thinking Washington would roll over were fooling themselves

The Cube, 8:37 p.m.
These teams are not good.

northenmich, 8:48 p.m.
this is brutal

monk11, 8:55 p.m.
Offensive play calling is atrocious so far

northenmich, 8:57 p.m.
that is so pathetic. [Michigan had failed to get a touchdown despite being near the end zone.]

northenmich, 8:59 p.m.
gonna blow this game doing stupid crap. unbelievable

ClarenceBoddicker, 9:01 p.m.
Our offense . . . isn't smart or good at all.

BHugh215, 9:06 p.m.
this is where we collapse and give up unnecessary points.

abertain, 9:14 p.m.
Can we delete the Corun [*sic*] hype? [The poster was implying that Blake Corum had been overrated in off-season coverage. Literally one minute later, at 9:15 p.m., Corum ran sixty-seven yards for the game's first touchdown.]

Brian Griese [not the real Brian Griese], 9:48 p.m.
That might be the all time worst series I have ever seen. [Michigan, though leading by ten, had run a play that seemingly called for McNamara, the quarterback, to run sideways and then fall down on third and seven. It really wasn't a good play.]

rice4114, 9:48 p.m.
What the fuck is going on?

ckersh74, 9:48 p.m.
What the actual fuck was THAT?!?

Mannix, 9:48 p.m.
What the hell is this.

abertain, 9:49 p.m.
I don't understand what's happening.

Ben Mathis-Lilley, the author of this book, in a DM to a
friend, 9:49 p.m.
what the fuck was that?

Boomer519, 9:51 p.m.
WTF, what the actual fuck?!?!

Bus3002, 9:57 p.m.
We're never going to even compete for the division with
Harbaugh. [At this point, Michigan scored twice, putting
the complaining briefly on pause, but later in the game,
Washington had a few good drives and scored a touchdown.]

JHumich, 10:29 p.m.
Horrible.

DuffyGoBlue, 10:46 p.m.
Jim Haurbugh [sic] is the biggest P*ssy in all of football!

JHUmich, 11:02 p.m.
We're going to get killed by any offense with a pulse.

Coldwater, 11:03 p.m.
piss poor secondary play is rearing it's [sic] ugly head. That
didn't get fixed from last year.

DuffyGoBlue, 11:03 p.m.
We will lose 3–5 games because we will not be able to throw
the ball when we're down to a team with a competent offense.
It's the same thing with this Harbaugh guy every year.

R.J. MacReady, 11:07 p.m.
Passing game is atrocious.

bigleo18, 11:08 p.m.
Crap azz play calling

Nofx1738, 11:09 p.m.
Horrible.

Blue19, 11:09 p.m.
This game has no right being this close.

fatpete,11:13 p.m.
What a fucking joke this program is . . .

lhglrkwg, 11:13 p.m.
We are not good.

Kyrand, 11:19 p.m.
Why can't we just put teams away. Harbaugh has no killer
instinct

Adrian, 11:33 p.m.
Never felt worse after a win.

uminks, 11:37 p.m.
Our [defensive] back field is pathetic

JHumich, 11:39 p.m.
Does anyone even fantasize that we can run like this in
Madison?

MichAtl85, 11:41 p.m.
[We] have a week maybe two to figure out how to pass the
football or finish 4th in the Big Ten East.

ScottMI-VA, 11:49 p.m.
we will get our doors blown off against a competent team

george11, 11:54 p.m.
This WIN will cost Michigan wins in the future due to a total
lack of QB and WR development.

AnthonyThomas, 11:58 p.m.
They didn't throw the ball because they're bad at it, and it's
going to result in losses down the road.

nowicki2005, 11:59 p.m.
Fire HARBAUGH.

———————◆———————

There is a brilliantly absurd relationship between these angry
messages and the reality that, as they were typed, Michigan was
scoring a convincing win over a well-known opponent on national
TV. It reminded me of a paper called "On Cooling the Mark Out,"
which was published in 1952 by a sociology professor named Erving Goffman. Goffman studied and theorized about the ways that
seemingly mundane, everyday interactions and events actually
speak to values and matters of social status that humans take
extremely seriously. "On Cooling the Mark Out" is about how con
artists go about handling a "mark" after they've conned them out
of their money, and how that's reminiscent of the way that individuals, organizations, and society as a whole handle people who've
lost face professionally, socially, and romantically.

The victim in a classic con, Goffman observed, is swindled out
of both money and his own sense that he's a savvy operator. (A colorful 1940 history of confidence scams called *The Big Con* served
as source material for both Goffman's article and the movie *The
Sting.*) "He has defined himself as a shrewd man and must face
the fact that he is only another easy mark," he writes. "He has
defined himself as possessing a certain set of qualities and then
proven to himself that he is miserably lacking in them." This is
the same sudden pulling of the rug that a person often experiences, Goffman observes, when they are fired, have an application
rejected, or are broken up with. In the old-timey con artist parlance, a mark who has had such an experience needs to be "cooled

out" so that they don't try to take revenge or otherwise lose their shit in a way that could draw the attention of legal authorities. In society, friends, peers, members of the clergy, therapists, and the like serve the same purpose as these coolers.

The fans reacting during Michigan's win over Washington—which was, in the scope of things, a routine and uneventful victory—were acting like marks who needed cooling out. They felt humiliation about the possibility that they didn't actually deserve a status they'd claimed for themselves—the status of "person affiliated with a successful, respected football team." They were also being reminded, in considering this possibility, of the humiliations that many disappointing Michigan football teams had put them through during previous games and seasons. The cooling-out or coping mechanism that they had created was to preemptively predict miserable results so as to prevent a more precipitous fall off the status cliff later on. "In case of failure," Goffman writes about a hypothetical subject attempting such a hedging strategy, "he can act as if the self that has failed is not one that is important to him." If you feign certainty in advance about how bad the team is going to be, you haven't lost anything when they turn out to be bad.

A number of the message board comments specifically disavowed Harbaugh. This is a dissociative move that allows a supporter to continue believing that Michigan still deserves the status that has been invested in it and that it has merely been failed by one individual person. (I think that's the "fall guy" technique in a con, in which the mark is led to believe that it was someone else's screw-up, not his own gullibility, that is responsible for his loss.) Of course, what it actually suggests is that fans' collective investment in Harbaugh was, at one point, quite significant as well.

A 1981 paper in the journal *Social Forces* called "Sport as Ritual" explains this a bit. The paper is by a now retired University of Iowa professor of "critical cultural studies" named Susan Birrell, whose official departmental photograph depicts her about to pitch a softball. She draws on Goffman's work but also on that of one of his inspirations, French theorist Émile Durkheim. Durkheim, in trying to figure out the common link between the many objects and places considered sacred by humans across the world, and operating under the assumption that it was probably not because they were all actually imbued with supernatural divine energy (sorry!), defined sacred things (in Birrell's words) as symbols of "the values which are special to the community and worthy of respect and reverence." Cultural rituals, he explained, are the means by which people pay tribute to those intangible values. You can't wear the concept of love, sacrifice, and redemption around your neck, but you can wear a cross, and so forth.

As Birrell explains, Goffman was especially interested in the way "action situations," like gambling and interpersonal confrontations, can demonstrate sacred values as well. During these occasions, individuals put their status and reputations on the line, and in so doing demonstrate socially revered qualities like courage, composure, "gameness" (by which he meant commitment and drive in the face of adversity), and "integrity" (not taking the easy way out). In times of challenge or crisis, people feel compelled to project certain qualities associated with their various social roles—Birrell lists "the loyal friend, the faithful lover, the loving parent, the efficient secretary, the dedicated scholar"—in a way that, in addition to making those individuals look good, reinforces to everyone that loyalty, parental love, and dedication to work are important.

These are the same kinds of values that religious texts and allegories seek to convey, and they are commonly cited as those that are imbued through participation in athletics. Birrell's insight is that they are hugely important to people who are watching sports as well. People explaining why they've become attached to a certain team or why they root for a certain athlete often cite their

virtues—the unity of purpose and mutual support that teammates evince, the fearlessness and strength of will shown by an
underdog, and so on. They put images of athletes on their walls, or
decorate them with team colors and symbols, similar to (and often
alongside) religious imagery, and they create game-day rituals
that parallel religious ones.

Birrell's position is that "the so-called 'hero worship' of athletes should not be regarded disparagingly as evidence of modern
man's replacement of religious ideals with secular or even heathen
images" and that "the shift does not mark a fundamental change
in social values but merely a substitution of the vessel in which
they are contained." In other words, it doesn't have to be shallow
idolatry to revere a sports figure. Those figures may legitimately
demonstrate a quality you find important, and if the concern is
that they are just running after a ball while wearing colorful uniforms, well, for all we really know, a priest may well just be a guy
wearing an unusual robe. (Sorry! My children are baptized! I'm
just saying, who knows?) Even people (like myself) who sometimes
think of themselves as being irritated by "moralizing" in sports
are often merely using their fandom to elevate alternative moral
values and heroes. Heretical *Moneyball* general manager Billy
Beane and St. Louis Cardinals labor pioneer Curt Flood come to
mind as examples of this, as does LeBron James, who has made
fans not only by being an excellent player but also by prioritizing
his economic autonomy and personal relationships with other
players over restrictive traditional norms that purportedly demonstrate loyalty and humility.

Goffman-style incentives exist for college football coaches,
who recruit local players and cultivate relationships with local
donors, to project locally valued traits. At South Carolina's Clemson University, evangelical Christian head coach Dabo Swinney
has built a powerful program in which many players are also
evangelicals, and the team has hosted at least one practice-field

player baptism. (Swinney and other representatives of Clemson, which is a public school, have said the football team welcomes players of all spiritual orientations and does not compel participation in any religious activity.) Pete Carroll won national titles at the University of Southern California in Los Angeles while smiling, chewing gum, hosting celebrities on the sideline, and generally somehow coaching a regimented, intense, and violent sport while appearing to always be taking it easy. And as I will discuss more during the visit to Baton Rouge in Chapter 7, Ed Orgeron's symbolic representation of Louisiana has been a source of both pride and chagrin to LSU fans.

Michigan fans had a lot of respect for Jim Harbaugh, exemplar of Michigan values, when he was hired in 2015. The big one, to be clear, was the value of winning football games or, to be more precise, the value of competence that he had demonstrated by winning them, given that he operates within a sphere in which everyone else also claims to really value winning. He went 29-6 as the head coach of the team at Division I-AA University of San Diego before starting at Stanford, where his record was even more impressive. The program historically hovers around .500 and was 1-11 the season before he started. By his fourth year, it went 12-1 and then won eleven, twelve, and eleven games, respectively, in the three years after he left, under his successor (David Shaw), whom Harbaugh had initially hired as an assistant. In those three years, Harbaugh was leading the NFL's 49ers, who had gone 6-10 the year before he started, to three straight appearances in the NFC conference championship game and one appearance in the Super Bowl. Harbaugh being a team's coach correlated strongly with a team getting better quickly, and this was something that Michigan, its athletic department, and its community were really excited about, because the team had been bad.

I wanted to know a bit more about this turnaround-artist reputation. The most commonly cited reason that teams become

successful under Harbaugh is that he imbues them with compet-
itiveness, which is a pretty abstract explanation, so I asked
former Stanford offensive tackle Ben Muth to make it more
comprehensible. Muth played his last two seasons at Stanford
under Harbaugh as the program's revival began, making the All-
Pac-12 team in his final year, and went on to become a professional writer for the Football Outsiders website. We spoke on the
phone while he was driving to an El Pollo Loco in Arizona for
lunch.

> I remember it started with winter conditioning. You do a
> bunch of agility drills, both conditioning and agility drills.
> He posted the results of those in the locker room. Where it
> really stood out, I remember, was our first spring ball on
> special teams. Special teams is supposed to be pretty much
> the whole team, but a lot of guys don't really want to mess
> around with it. After the first week of practice, the coaches
> announced, "All right, here's who competed in this many
> special teams drills. This is how they did." It was really
> noticeable that certain guys didn't get out there. He called
> them out on it.

General demeanor was also a factor. "There's certain tangible
stuff, but it really felt like it was just a big attitude change. You
knew what he expected of you, and there were high expectations,"
he said. Muth got a flavor for this even before workouts started.

> I was at the Cotton Bowl in Dallas right after they
> announced that they hired him. Just there as a fan. I must
> have been wearing some Stanford stuff or something,
> because some guy came up to me, some kid came up to me,
> and was like, "Oh, I saw you guys hired Harbaugh," blah
> blah blah—"He's an asshole." I was like, "Oh, really?" I
> think he had gone to Drake or Dayton, somewhere that

had played USD [the University of San Diego], and I guess USD had really run the score up on them that year. The coach came over to him after the game and was basically like, "What the fuck, Jim?" Jim allegedly—and this is secondhand knowledge—Jim allegedly blew up on him, like, "It's not my job to stop us. It's *your* job to stop us." That was really the first thing I had heard about Harbaugh as a coach. I remember liking it.

(San Diego did beat Drake, in Iowa, 37-0 in 2006. No one currently employed at Drake or USD's athletic department could confirm the story, but Harbaugh has been party to two other infamous midfield postgame confrontations, one with USC's Carroll and one with the Detroit Lions' Jim Schwartz.) Former Michigan tight end Jake Butt told the Big Ten Network in 2016 that Harbaugh had demonstrated a particular type of basic block on his own lectern in a meeting room, repeating it and becoming more and more animated until he smashed it off its bearings, across the room, and into a wall.

Harbaugh also understood the program's past without being limited by it. He had succeeded as a coach with teams that ran the ball more than they passed, which is becoming less common in college football and is very rare in the NFL. But the way those teams ran the ball was novel. Offensive linemen and tight ends lined up in unusual places and pulled in unusual directions after the snap. Sometimes the quarterback handed off, but sometimes he faked a handoff and kept it. Harbaugh embodied toughness and strength and steadfastness and all that stuff, but also savvy and relevance, the latter two qualities having become more and more rare around the Michigan program as the twenty-first century went on. Tradition, but not obsolescence.

He was also, by the standards of sport, a public intellectual, albeit a hard one to pin down. Since becoming Michigan's coach, he has written a short item praising Colin Kaepernick for *Time* magazine, said on a National Review podcast that he deplores the prevalence of abortion, met with Barack Obama and invited him to be an honorary captain at a football game, announced that he would show the football team Clint Eastwood's red-state hit *American Sniper* after a screening elsewhere on campus was canceled, cited both Malcolm X and militarist 1951–1978 Ohio State coach Woody Hayes as inspirations for a pair of new black-rimmed glasses, and made multiple Washington, DC, appearances on behalf of the Legal Services Corporation, a federally funded legal-aid nonprofit. He also used donor funds to take the team on spring trips to Rome (where he met the pope), France, and South Africa. (The university reversed its decision to cancel the *Sniper* screening, and, per the *Michigan Daily*, Harbaugh met privately with Middle Eastern, North African, Muslim, and South Asian students at the student union to discuss the controversy.)

If there's a common thread there, it's an old-fashioned idea of patriotic but inclusive Americanness, an enthusiasm for achievement, self-expression, and possibility. (Ace Anbender, a very funny and insightful writer who produces a newsletter called *The Bucket Problem* about Michigan sports, calls it admiration for "Real Men of Action.") It doesn't fit into one of our dominant present-day ideological groupings but probably would have done well as a presidential campaign message for either major party in about 1956. (The implied admiration of Malcolm X would have been a liability.) To be clear, he was and is someone who is obsessed with winning and football. But he has an awareness of the wider world that to me seems unlike a football coach.

Muth disagreed when I phrased the issue to him in that way. "No, no, no. I think the difference is what you consider a football coach and what Jim Harbaugh considers a football coach are different things. To Coach Harbaugh, a football coach is a spiritual mentor. It's a teacher. It's life in general. He truly believes a football coach can probably do more good than maybe anyone in the country, except for the president."

He was saying I had it backward: Harbaugh isn't a well-rounded person who coaches football but rather someone who is so serious about coaching football that he feels it incumbent upon himself to be well-rounded so as to be able to pass that on to his players. Said Muth, "I think he likes coaching at Stanford, and USD is a great academic school, and Michigan, because he thinks part of being a good football coach is making sure your guys are good students. He thinks that's just part of the job. He thinks making them into good men is part of the job."

Before the 2015 season started, Harbaugh's first at Michigan, a reporter asked him if the attention on the team was overwhelming to players. He responded, "You want to be at that big-boy table—big persons table, might be better to say. There's another table over there in the kitchen for those people that aren't seated at that big person's table. If someone wants to go over there, no one's going to be upset if they do. But this is what we signed up for, this is what I signed up for, and I know a lot of our players did." Ambitious, yes, robustly so, but sensitive to changing notions of gender equity. It was all a good fit for a school that wants to rival Ohio State in the field of hitting things and Harvard in the field of advancing the human condition.

For Muth, this is easily traced to Jim's father, Jack, who raised his family while working as a football assistant at Michigan and Stanford. Jack later had a long stint as the head coach at Western Kentucky, which culminated in a Division I-AA championship. Willie Taggart, the subject of Chapter 9, played for the elder Harbaugh at WKU and was an assistant coach there during its championship season.

"I think the first time his dad spoke to the team, that's when things clicked into place for me," Muth said. "Jim's just an evolved model of Jack. If you've ever talked to him or heard him talk for more than five minutes, you know his dad was absolutely his hero. He didn't just see his dad as someone who went off to coach football. He saw his dad as the man who raised him." The best parking spot outside Schembechler Hall is reserved for Jack Harbaugh. (The sign just says "Jack.") He went on,

> What I would say, and just kind of summarize my thoughts on Jim, is, he's said it multiple times, and the first time I heard him say it, I laughed, but now I know this is 100 percent who he is as a person. He said, "I figured my life out when I was six years old. You play football for as long as you can. You coach football for as long as you can. Then you die." That is 100 percent what he wants to do. If it goes bad at Michigan, he'll take another job, whether it's in the NFL or in college. He'll stay there if he likes it for as long as possible, and if it's not going good, he'll take a smaller job. It would not shock me if Jim Harbaugh is eighty-five years old coaching some small Catholic high school in whatever town he happens to be living in.

For some period of time, in fact, it had been conjectured that Michigan administrators wouldn't want to bring Harbaugh on as a coach because he'd said in 2007 that the university didn't take academics seriously enough relative to Stanford. "College football needs Stanford," he said then. "We're looking not for student-athletes, but *scholar*-athletes." He told the *Ann Arbor News* in a follow-up interview that he'd been told not to major in history as a U of M undergrad because it would take up too much time.

The Michigan football team's NCAA-tracked graduation success rate (GSR) in the most recent data set was 96 percent, only one percentage point below Northwestern among Big Ten teams (and higher, in this one year at least, than Stanford). The regular contributors on the 2021 team—that is, players who actually saw playing time on the field—included majors in political science, English, African American studies, economics, and mechanical engineering. Harbaugh-era defensive lineman Carlo Kemp (political science major, business minor) told me that in the program, "being in class was something that was talked about all the time." And not merely being present: "That you were participating, that you were active in it." (For the sake of comparison, Louisiana State's GSR has never been above 78 percent in any of the seventeen years the NCAA has data for.)

None of what I have conveyed so far quite captures the Jim Harbaugh experience, though. He simply broadcasts on a different frequency than the rest of us. Said one person I spoke to, "I don't think he's like anything else, even in his own family. I've met John, and I met Jack Sr., and they're pretty normal. Jack Harbaugh is a normal grandpa. Is he a football coach grandpa? Yes. But he's a pretty normal guy. John's the same way. Jim is just wired so differently, in even his own family."

Harbaugh was famous in San Francisco for wearing Walmart khakis, but in 2016, he switched to a blue Lululemon model. ("You don't want to become like stale bread, overripe fruit, or burnt meat," he said of the change.) During the 2021 season, against Penn State (see Chapter 10), his Lululemons caught on fire because he didn't notice how close he was standing to a space heater. Afterward, he gave a rare public rebuke of a player, wide receiver Daylen Baldwin, who he said had not been forceful enough in telling him his pants were on fire. "I made a little coaching point to Daylen Baldwin—if somebody's on fire, man—'Hey. Coach.' Maybe just grab me and get me out of the way or something, you know? Be a little more emphatic about the fact that somebody's on fire."

From a distance, Harbaugh might seem like he lacks a sense of humor or irony, but that's not quite it. During the Western Michigan game, freshman backup quarterback J. J. McCarthy improvised during several plays with sometimes disastrous results. Afterward, Harbaugh observed that McCarthy is not "a victim of overcoaching," which is, I think, a little funny. What's going on, rather, is that he never calibrates his demeanor or opinion because it might create a backlash, and he never says what a person is "supposed to" say in a given social situation. He's decided who Jim Harbaugh, Football Coach, is going to be, how he's going to act, and what he's going to care about, and that's that. If he decides he doesn't have anything to say at a certain time, he stops talking rather than filling the air, which can be awkward.

Says Muth,

> Your first impression, it's weird, because he's almost such a cliché of a football coach, but it seems kind of full of shit at first. I think the longer you're around him, it's like, oh, no, this is who he is. He comes in, and he talks a big game about what he's going to do and what we're going to do as a team, but he backs it up. He lives it. I don't think he's ever said something that he didn't really and truly believe. I think the most recent thing I heard was, "Beat Ohio State or die trying." [Harbaugh had, in fact, said this at Big Ten Media Day in July 2021.] It's one of those things where it's a cliché, but I 100 percent believe that's how Jim Harbaugh feels. He would stay at Michigan until he beats Ohio State or dies, if it's entirely up to him.

———◦———

I have seen this clarity of purpose in action. In June 2016, Harbaugh and other Michigan staff members were doing a tour of football camps for high school players around the country—long practices, essentially, but without pads on and focused on the more fun, competitive kinds of drills. One was held in suburban Paramus, New Jersey. I was already trying to scheme up some way to

write about him, so I borrowed a friend's minivan and drove there
to observe.

It was an unusual opportunity to see someone of his notoriety
up close, because the media side of the event was run by the high
school, Paramus Catholic, and they didn't have either the man-
power or the inclination to put as many parts of it as possible
off-limits, which seems to be what college and pro teams (and anyone else who handles celebrities) regard as the best way to handle
things. So I got to follow around Harbaugh and a bunch of other
coaches from Michigan and a number of other schools for several
hours in the parking lot, hallways, cafeteria, and such. The event
was open to any college that wanted to send staff members, and
there were head coaches from other major-conference programs
present too. Generally, there were a lot of extremely large men in
circulation with intensity in their brows and bone-crushing
strength in their grips. (Football coaches were once football players, and football players are big. This was somehow not something
I had put together before seeing it in person; I had expected, I
guess, that when they went from playing into the white-collar
profession of coaching, they would shrink to regular size. This is
possibly because they look small on TV next to players wearing
pads and helmets. Anyway.)

Harbaugh, despite being a relatively slight figure by the standards of the day, was its center of energy. The high school kids, a
group of a few hundred, had assembled in the gym before the
practice started. A head coach from another school welcomed
them and gave a pep talk about effort, hard work, and so forth. It
was pretty standard stuff. Then Harbaugh spoke, and he began
by describing, if I recall, something he'd read or heard about the
way a horse's heartbeat can be seen through its skin as it's preparing to run the Kentucky Derby. It was a visceral account. There
may have been something about the physical size of the organ,
maybe something about sweat. And it went on for a while. His
point, he ultimately said, was that this was how excited he felt

any time he got the chance to be on a football field, and it was how excited he was, that minute, to be at a practice for teenagers in New Jersey.

When everyone got to the field, he proved his point, putting himself in charge of dividing the players into heats for sprint competitions, acting as the starter for each race, and declaring and congratulating the winners. A man in his element. After a while, I walked to the middle of the field for a better angle on the "finish line," which was marked by an assistant standing with his arms outstretched. Or at least I thought it was an assistant. When I got closer, I realized that the low-key human traffic cone was Jim's brother John, who had won the Super Bowl as head coach of the Baltimore Ravens. He and a few other Ravens staffers had come up to help out. No one in the crowd of aspiring NFL players and football reporters had noticed him yet. He looked amused.

John also figured in a Harbaugh story I heard from former Michigan safety Josh Metellus, who as of the time of this writing plays for the Minnesota Vikings. Metellus is from South Florida and said that one of his first interactions with his college coach was an in-home recruiting visit involving two of his other high school teammates who also went on to attend U of M. Jim arrived in a car driven by John, who had just coached the Ravens in a game against the Dolphins in Miami. John dropped Jim off as if he were a fifteen-year-old arriving at a friend's house. Then Jim and the three teenagers played the card game Spades for several hours, and that was the entire recruiting visit. Metellus said Harbaugh paid close attention to the outcome of each hand. "I loved it," he said. "I was like, if our head coach is this competitive, we're going to win games."

The possibility of winning big with this kind of distinctive and distinctly Michiganian value-embodiment had people pretty worked up. Chris Partridge had been a high school head coach (at Paramus Catholic, actually) and an assistant at two smaller college programs when Harbaugh hired him on to Michigan's staff in 2015. In 2021, he was forty-one years old and working as the defensive coordinator at Ole Miss. "People were really, really excited," Partridge said about the early days. "It was a huge, way bigger environment than I had been involved in. When you're in the football building, and you're trying to get stuff done, that environment gets shrunk. But every time we left the building, there were people standing outside trying to get Jim's autograph, trying to find out which way he's leaving."

But as Harbaugh's teams on the field wobbled and then collapsed in 2020, his character traits were reinterpreted as flaws. You can see it in the comments about the Washington game. Michigan finished that contest with fifty-six rushing attempts to only fifteen passes, which is a preposterous ratio, even in the Big Ten. This kind of imbalance, so enraging to Thicc Stauskas, was said to be a consequence of Harbaugh's obsession with individual character and aggression and was proof that the team wouldn't be able to pass if it ever needed to. His diversity of interests, creative energy, and fixation on fundamentals (trips abroad, complicated plays, blocking lecterns into walls, etc.), in reverse polarity, constituted disorganization, a short attention span, and an inability to prioritize. (The team did, in fact, often seem confused on the field, with the offense failing to snap the ball in time and the defense in turn failing to get itself set up properly when the opposing offense played quickly.) His directness and lack of guile became an unwillingness to form and manage the necessary relationships with players and others at the university.

This last one was a big one. Before the 2021 season, the Wolverine Digest website calculated that sixty players had transferred out of the Michigan program since 2018, one of the highest numbers in the Big Ten and twice as many as had left rivals Ohio State and Michigan State in the same period. Twenty-one had left in the previous year, the most in the conference. Some had been

well-regarded recruits and on-field contributors at positions where
the team could have used them, particularly on the offensive and
defensive lines. Fans complained that top prospects were alien-
ated by Harbaugh's inflexibility and that top offensive players in
particular avoided Michigan because of the aforementioned
running-game fixation. A number of the best football prospects
in the state of Michigan came out of a Detroit-area high school
named Belleville; they had stopped attending U of M, going
instead to programs like Michigan State, Penn State, and Kentucky, for reasons that neither Harbaugh nor Belleville's head
coach explained.

What frustrated Alex, Thicc Stauskas, and the substantial
group of people who agreed with them was the idea of being associated with an institution that was both arrogant and dumb. Matt
Campbell, the Iowa State coach, was a perfect foil: He was from
Ohio, did not have elite educational credentials, was said to have
great relationships across the region, and carried himself with the
relentlessly positive attitude of a church youth group leader. He
was, or was imagined to be, someone nice and humble enough to
do the easy, smart thing.

Some of the people I spoke to confirmed the long-discussed
allegation that Harbaugh can "rub people the wrong way." Said
Metellus, "There was a lot of times as a team we bumped heads,
and there wasn't a lot of slack given on his end. It was his way or no
way." I made a comment about the coach seeming like "a pretty
intense dude" to be around. "Yeah," he said. "Especially for four
years."

I also spoke to the mother of former Michigan wide receiver
Donovan Peoples-Jones, Roslyn Peoples, who became known as an
advocate for players' rights vis-à-vis the NCAA when her son was
in high school. Peoples-Jones was an elite prospect at Cass Tech
High School in Detroit and has become a big-play threat for the
NFL's Cleveland Browns, but he caught only thirty-four passes in

his last season at Michigan (2019), which is not that many for a player of NFL-caliber talent. I asked Peoples if her experience with Harbaugh's program had been a positive one. "Well, now, there's a politically correct answer, and I've been trained if you can't say anything good, just don't say anything," she said. I prompted her with the idea that the coach specifically overburdened his players because he feels that they should be 4.0 GPA superhumans at the same time they're winning Big Ten titles. "I will say that a lot of their players had hamstring injuries," she offered. (Peoples-Jones was frequently listed on injury reports as having a strained groin, which could have been the result of overwork.)

Muth is a big fan of Harbaugh's but explained to me how his relationship with players can sour:

> If he thought you were doing things right on the football field, he loved you. If you weren't, and he thought you could do things better, he let you know about it. The relationship could get frustrating. Something that may be a very small detail to another coach is a big deal to him. He's a detail guy a lot of the times on the football field—what your stance should look like, this is how a cadence sounds if you're a quarterback, all of that. Sometimes guys may not necessarily agree that that's the most important thing, and you feel like you're being picked on because your bad habit just happened to be a pet peeve of the head coach. But he has a lot of pet peeves. He's going to let you know about it, and it's not going to be fun until you get it corrected.

The best theory of the 2020 season I was able to develop is that Harbaugh had accumulated too many assistant coaches who were a bit too much like him in this way. That year's team was "wildly burned out," one person who was around the program at the time said to me. Defensive coordinator Don Brown, sixty-seven years old, was described to me as "inflexible" and a "his way or the highway" kind of ol' cuss. Cornerbacks coach Mike Zordich (who was fifty-nine years old and had played 185 games in the NFL) had "pissed off all of Detroit" for saying former star and city native Lavert Hill needed to "learn to play with some nicks" instead of sitting out practice. (This had happened in 2018. Said the source, "Detroit . . . they hold grudges.") Regarding offensive line coach Ed Warinner, a sixty-year-old football lifer from rural Ohio, "No one liked him. No one liked him, at all." Those three coaches were replaced after the year with younger and purportedly more "relatable" ones.

However, I was surprised to find that no one within the football world whom I talked to, on or off the record, was as critical as fans were about Harbaugh's capabilities or demeanor, or how they affected his chances of turning the ship around. After all, it is the rare football coach who doesn't wear on a certain number of the dozens and dozens of players he's in charge of each year. "For the most part, I felt like he did a good job," Metellus said, later adding, "He's the head coach, so it *is* his way or no way. Anybody is going to bump heads if you're with each other for that long." Acker, a players' rights advocate whose job in some respects is to be skeptical of Michigan's administration, said he was confident that "the academic side and the health and safety and success of the players" was being handled appropriately (and that it had been the reason Manuel retained Harbaugh despite the poor 2020 season record). "Jim is a winner," Partridge said. "He's always been a winner, and he still is a winner."

Said Muth, "One thing about college is there is a lot of turnover from year to year. The guys that are coming into the program are guys that decide to play for him. There's always going to be some level of buy-in on a college team. I think it can turn around. It would not shock me if they had a good year." I asked him if he thought Harbaugh's subdued, almost introverted public demeanor of late was a sign that he'd lost his enthusiasm for the job. He said,

> I think Jim is a guy that doesn't necessarily feel like he's earned the right to take shots at Ohio State when he hasn't beat Ohio State. I don't think Jim's ever been one for idle trash talk. I think he talked trash before, when he'd first gotten the job, before he had a chance to back it up, because he truly believed he was going to back it up. I think he feels guilty right now throwing any barbs at Ohio State, because he feels like he hasn't earned it. I think if Michigan goes 11-1 this year and beats Ohio State, I think he will let people know that it was a job well done.

INTERLUDE

Jim Harbaugh, on the Monday after Michigan's victory over Washington, on the disparity between the team's number of rushing attempts and passing attempts:

Heard a little bit of noise about, "Why so much running? Are you gonna throw more?" That kind of thing. We all know there are a lot of ways to travel. Some people choose to travel on the ground; some people by air. George Patton was able to get his job done on the ground. Neil Armstrong, through the air. Last Saturday night, we chose to grind it out on the ground. And we were also able to get our mission accomplished.

CHAPTER

6

WISCONSIN AND
NEBRASKA

ELEVEN AND ONE? It was far-fetched. Michigan had won that many games only twice in the preceding twenty-three seasons. There were fans and members of the Michigan football community who supported Jim Harbaugh's retention in 2021—if everyone had agreed with Thicc Stauskas, he wouldn't have had to tell someone they had a baby brain—but even in this group, there was often a fatalism about the program's so-called ceiling. The line one often heard was that Jim cared more about the university than anyone else in his position would, and it was telling that his supporters operated on a first-name basis. It spoke to a sense that it was better to do as well as possible with a member of the family, as it were, than to instigate a bitter divorce and then do the same or worse on the field. "He's a good coach, good to great coach, and who else are you going to hire that's better than him?" one person in the program's orbit said to me before the 2021 season. "People should understand that he is the best that they're going to get." Hell yeah! Let's fuckin' go!

As little as that sentiment got one hyped and jacked up, it was true that circumstances were conspiring against the program and its coach. The team's two biggest games of the midseason period, October 2 and October 9 road games against Wisconsin and Nebraska, respectively, were helpful for understanding how and why.

After running over Washington, Michigan had hammer-jacked Northern Illinois 63-10 and beat Rutgers 20-13 (uncomfortably close, but it happened after U of M led 20-3 at halftime and, we can now say with hindsight, endured some essentially random growing-pain mishaps during the second half that resulted in the close score). Its body of work was strong. The rock was still being pounded with vigor and efficiency, but McNamara and the receivers had been interspersing long touchdown throws. The defensive line and secondary had been sturdy, competent, and trustworthy, the kind of position groups you'd want taking out your daughter (or son!). Senior defensive end Aidan Hutchinson kept sacking people and building the team's ineffable but important quotient of momentum-compounding swag. (Asked to describe the experience of hitting Western Michigan's quarterback while stripping the ball out of his hands for a fumble, Hutchinson—wearing his hair gelled back, aviator shades, and a gold chain over an open collar, a Patrick Swayze for the new century—responded that "it was fun.")

Heading into Wisconsin week, though, Wolverine supporters were still queasy. A writer named Alex Kirshner published an article on the numbers-oriented FiveThirtyEight website called "The Case for Believing in Michigan Football." He began by noting that "Michigan football fans are not conditioned in their modern state to feel anything good," and then he preemptively apologized on social media for maybe having jinxed everything. Why? Primarily it was because of something that I will call the Hated Self-Reinforcing Graphic of Despair. Below is the version of the Graphic of Despair that was aired during the 2020 Michigan–Penn State game.

To see why this graphic was so ubiquitous and frustrating, you have to start by going back about fifty years, to 1970, at which point historically all-white southern universities were finally integrating their teams, inaugurating the modern era. It was Michigan football's best decade of said era, in which the team won a double-digit number of games seven times. The baby boom concurrently drove enrollment at the university to almost triple its prewar level, so a lot of people were moving through and watching a winning football team. The modern Michigan fan base and its sense of how successful the program should be were created in the '70s. It is that baseline against which Harbaugh was being judged by the Graphic of Despair. Here are the final 1970 AP rankings:

1. Nebraska
2. Notre Dame
3. Texas

4. Tennessee

5. Ohio State

6. Arizona State

7. LSU

8. Stanford

9. Michigan

10. Auburn

11. Arkansas

12. Toledo

13. Georgia Tech

14. Dartmouth

15. USC

16. Air Force

17. Tulane

18. Penn State

19. Houston

20. (tie) Ole Miss and Oklahoma

Four of the top twelve teams (look at little Toledo getting it done!) were within a triangular chunk of the Midwest running from South Bend to Ann Arbor to Columbus, an area that constitutes roughly 0.36 percent of the landmass of the continental United States. The top team was Nebraska. Dartmouth was on there, somehow. The South was represented, but not disproportionately so.

Fifty years later, in 2020, Alabama won the national championship again. Five of the top seven teams—Alabama, Clemson, Texas A&M, Oklahoma, and Georgia—in the final AP poll were southern, by the US Census Bureau definition. Between 1970 and 1995, there were seventeen national championships claimed by schools outside the South; between 1996 and 2020, there were six.

What happened over that fifty-year period is that people moved to the South, many of them from the Midwest, a process that was already underway by 1970 and remains ongoing. In that year, Ohio and Michigan—the two main states from which U of M has traditionally drawn its players, as Jordan Acker alluded to—constituted almost 10 percent of the US population. The Midwest and South (as defined by the Census Bureau) were of comparable size: 57 million people and 63 million people, respectively. In 2020, there were 69 million Americans in the Midwest and 126 million in the South. In 1970, Cuyahoga County, Ohio—which includes Cleveland—had the same population, 1.7 million, as Harris County, Texas, which includes Houston. Today, those numbers are 1.3 million for Cuyahoga County and 4.7 million for Harris County. Michigan and Ohio are one-third smaller than they used to be as a share of the national population.

The large-scale population divergence of the Midwest and the South may have actually gotten less attention in the regular news media, where narratives focus more on the growth and decline of specific cities, than in college football circles, where generation-defining demographic patterns are better understood—if not always by more casual fans or TV producers creating graphics about a coach's allegedly poor performance—because they affect whether your team can "pull in a top-ten class." There are a few reasons I've seen or heard to explain the overall trend:

> *The rise of air-conditioning.* Between 1960 and 1980, per a frequently cited 1984 paper by a professor at the University of South Florida, the number of southern households that had some kind of air-conditioning grew from less than a quarter to well over half. Now, almost all of them have it. A University of New Hampshire demographer named Ken Johnson noted to me that even the, uh, person-creating process itself may have changed because of AC. "There's some evidence that it played a part in fertility patterns," Johnson said. "That is, when babies were born changed once air-conditioning began to become available. Nine months after August was not as big

a time for babies to be born in the South prior to air-conditioning."

The relocation of manufacturing jobs. The spread of air-conditioning also correlated with an increase in the number of factories built in warmer areas; the scale of the units required initially meant that AC was common in workplaces before homes. Textile production had already shifted almost entirely from New England to the South by the 1950s, something that was attributed to anti-union laws and low local minimum wages by critics including New England college football fan and senator John F. Kennedy, who wrote (or "wrote") an article about these purported "unfair practices" for the *Atlantic* in 1954. The trend has since been replicated in other industries: between 1980 and 2013, per a figure I found in the *American Prospect*, the number of auto industry jobs in the Midwest fell by 33 percent, while those in the South—where unionization is still rare—increased by 52 percent.

The end of Jim Crow. The "Great Migration" of Black Americans to the North—generally attributed to the superior economic opportunities and (relatively) progressive civil rights environment in cities like Detroit—lasted from the late nineteenth century until about 1975. Since then, the trend has reversed, with the Black population in Atlanta, for example, doubling between 1990 and 2020.

A cartoon mouse. Disney, which we will return to shortly, opened its Orlando theme park in 1971, when the city had a population of 331,000. It's now more than 2 million.

Bud Elliott is a Florida native and University of Alabama law school graduate—"I had a good LSAT day and got lucky," he says—who has since moved into the more honorable field of college football analysis for the 247Sports network. He once said on

Twitter that he would prefer not to ever be outside in a temperature less than fifty degrees, and he is one of the country's leading
experts on football recruiting in the South (and everywhere else).
He is known for having observed that no team with a "blue-chip
ratio" of less than 50 percent—that is, a roster of scholarship players that's less than half made up of athletes who were given ratings
of four or five stars (out of a potential five) by evaluators at the
major recruiting services, the details of that process being too
arcane even for this book—has won a national championship since
at least 2002. As Elliott told me,

> I was at all these recruiting camps and then seeing the
> type of players that certain teams were signing, from a
> physical perspective. And then I was having difficulty
> squaring what I knew about what they were signing, these
> different teams across the country, and the type of player
> and the number of the type of players that they were sign-
> ing of that high caliber, and squaring that with the narra-
> tive that other teams were going to compete for and
> ultimately win the national title. I started to just kind of
> back-test some stuff, and it probably would not have gone
> anywhere, except for I just got to a really nice round num-
> ber and said, 'Oh, wow, okay.' People can understand that
> you need to have more than half of your previous four sign-
> ing classes be four- and five-star recruits.

College football is a big business but a local game. Most players, like most college students in general, stay fairly close to home.
(Acker was in the stadium tunnel while the Southern Methodist
University team left the field after losing to Michigan in 2018. "I
want an energy bar, and I want to see my mom," he overheard one
of its players saying.) By my count, fourteen of the starters on Alabama's 2020 national championship team were listed with a hometown in the state or one that borders it. (The number of "starters"

on a modern football team can vary depending on how one counts certain players with specialized roles, but it's in the neighborhood of twenty-five.)

Heading into 2021, eight of the nine top teams by blue-chip ratio (including Orgeron's LSU) were in the South. The only nonsouthern school was Ohio State, which was third. Michigan was tenth. Southern schools are known for more lenient academic and disciplinary standards, and for sometimes arranging for their supposedly amateur players to be paid. But the fact of the matter is that the warmer part of the country is where most of the good football players are to begin with. By my count, sixty-nine of the top one hundred individuals on 247Sports' list of the most talented players in the high school class of 2022 were from the South. Ranked opponents from the Graphic of Despair that had given Michigan the business included talent-heavy southern teams such as Alabama, Florida State (before Taggart worked there), and Florida. (There was also Ohio State, which has embraced a certain set of buttery, chicken-fried cultural practices regarding recruiting and player eligibility that I will address later in an objective and nonjudgmental manner.)

A comprehensive list of reasons why Jim Harbaugh didn't have Michigan's program in the same position as Bo Schembechler did would include the Civil Rights Act of 1964 and Henry Galson's development of the affordable window-unit air conditioner in the 1940s. Before the team's collapse in 2020, by most measures, Michigan had been one of the ten or so best teams in the country under Harbaugh, in aggregate. It'd been closer to the tenth best than the best, though. As a Michigan beat reporter named Isaiah Hole noticed before the 2020 season, nine of the losses to ranked teams that the graphic saddled Harbaugh with, including seven of the "top ten" losses, took place when Michigan was lower ranked than its opponent. Which is generally when you're supposed to lose.

So there was a very accusatory graphic that purported to depict epic failure but in fact showed a guy doing maybe a little worse, but not that much worse, than he could be expected to do given the historical context. That it was so inescapable speaks to some other unfortunate trends.

The media, to summarize things, is in an even more desperate and craven state than usual. To use the same cutoff as before, daily newspaper circulation in the United States in 1970 was 62 million, according to the Pew Research Center. In 2020, it was 24 million. That's despite the country's population having risen from about 200 million to 330 million in the intervening half a century. Readers have gone online, but their money hasn't followed them: paid online subscriptions are hard to sell, while Facebook, Google, and Amazon receive a mind-boggling 64 percent of all digital advertising spending, by one estimate. Total newspaper ad revenue, again according to Pew, has fallen from around $50 billion to an estimated $9 billion in the last fifteen years. According to the *Washington Post*, 2,200 local newspapers have closed since 2005, and per the *Financial Times*, more than half of the ones that still do exist are owned by financial firms that do not necessarily have long-term sustainability in mind, most prominently one called Alden Global Capital. The *Atlantic* recently described Alden's business model like so: "Gut the staff, sell the real estate, jack up subscription prices, and wring as much cash as possible out of the enterprise until eventually enough readers cancel their subscriptions that the paper folds, or is reduced to a desiccated husk of its former self."

Online-only news sites like the one I work for, *Slate*, have not grown nearly fast enough to make up the ground lost by print publications. There were about eighty thousand combined "newsroom" employees in the country between newspapers and the internet in 2008, according to Pew, but that number fell to forty-nine thousand by 2020. Layoffs, instability, and constant job-related fear are the status quo for life in this particular sector, according to an industry insider (me). Many of the positions that are still available, as you may have noticed even if you aren't a member of the press, involve pressure to quickly repackage other publications' articles in the most sensational and provocative ways possible to make up traffic (readership, clicks, etc.) on the cheap. Because of smartphones and the internet, news is much more available around the clock to readers now than it used to be. But at the same time, there is also less actual news, in the form of things people find out and then report on, because there are fewer people doing those things.

In the sports world, the evolution of *Sports Illustrated* is an indicative case. Once a weekly Time Inc. publication with an illustrious national reporting staff and a circulation of 3.2 million, it now distributes seventeen issues a year to around half as many alleged subscribers and is controlled by a company that in the past three years has been called TheMaven, Maven, and The Arena Group. The Arena Group has retained some of the publication's best writers, including several who I hope will compliment and help promote this book. It also uses the SI brand name as an umbrella for a "digital family" that includes team-specific sites of wildly varying quality run by modestly paid contributors who do a lot of content repackaging. These team-specific proprietors, according to reporting that was done by the sports site Deadspin shortly before a private equity company drove off and replaced its entire staff, were once told that if they needed help writing more posts, they should find local college students to do them for free. As I'm writing this, the top news item on SI.com is a 217-word article that cites other outlets' work four times and reads like it was translated from Bulgarian by a computer (e.g., "In late November, NBA reporter Marc Stein also noted how there was increasing buzz in coaching circles about increasing pressure on [Frank] Vogel.")

Now, you might be saying to yourself, "The media is not just writers, you self-centered idiot. What about television, the thing that normal people care about?" That's fair. TV is more important than words. What's really messed up is that this is happening in that part of the industry too, even though it still makes a lot of money! In part because of the decline of every kind of printed-word competition, ESPN, which is part of Disney's cultural omni-conglomerate along with Pixar, Marvel, Lucasfilm (i.e., Star Wars), and the studio formerly known as 20th Century Fox, is by far the biggest sports media entity, with some competition from Fox Sports (which is, confusingly, no longer related to 20th Century Fox). It's definitely the biggest college football media entity, having, for example, broadcast forty-one of 2021's forty-four bowl games. The "Worldwide Leader" employs some of the best reporters and commentators in the industry, almost by definition, but is getting rid of them at an alarming rate. About one hundred newsroom contributors, including some of the best-known and most knowledgeable in their sports, were terminated in a single day in 2017. Several more were laid off or not offered new contracts during the pandemic. The *60 Minutes*–style news show *Outside the Lines*, which used to air every day, was cut to once a week.

The company has filled their absence with hot takes, running five hours of talk shows on a typical weekday. Seemingly all of them feature one personality, Stephen A. Smith, giving opinions at an insane level of hyperbole. The most recent position on Smith's Twitter timeline as I'm writing this is, "I think it would be a disaster if the NETS won the CHAMPIONSHIP!" Okay. The next one is, "This FRANCHISE"—the Dallas Cowboys, I think—"is a DAMN DISGRACE!" Journalism!

About five years ago, meanwhile, Fox Sports laid off nearly all its writers and reporters and poached the top producer of ESPN's hot-take shows, Jamie Horowitz, as well as some of its non–Stephen A. Smith pundits, to create six daily hours of men-arguing-with-each-other programming. (Horowitz has since left the company, but his business model persists.) When I wrote an article about Fox Sports in 2017, longtime ESPN personality Colin

Cowherd, who'd signed a big contract to switch networks, had taken seven different positions about NFL quarterback Jimmy Garoppolo, who was at the time Tom Brady's backup on the New England Patriots, in the span of five months. (First he said the Patriots should trade Brady, then that they should trade Garoppolo to rebuild their team around Brady, then that they needed to keep Garoppolo because Brady might be washed up, then that Garoppolo should be traded to the Cleveland Browns, then that they needed to keep Garoppolo because Brady was too inconsistent, then that they had the leverage to trade Garoppolo for a huge return because Brady performed so well in the Super Bowl, and finally that they would be foolish to trade Garoppolo because Brady would be retiring soon.) Jason Whitlock, also an ESPN expat, did a segment about his belief that Colin Kaepernick is an activist because he feels bad about being adopted by white parents.

Cowherd once noted, in a sort of admirably honest interview with Bryan Curtis of the Ringer, that "in my business, being absolutely, absurdly wrong occasionally is a wonderful thing," said he constantly tells one of his friends in the industry that "there's no money in right," and concluded a rumination about whether he'd been wrong about the subject of that day's show—his accusation that a particular quarterback, whose race you may be able to guess correctly, didn't prepare enough for games—by asking, "Who cares?"

So sports fans (and everyone else) are dealing with a media whose ascendant business model is getting viewers and readers worked up as often as possible—if necessary, by knowingly making arguments that might be wrong. As dumb as that sounds when said out loud, it's probably a smart strategy from a financial perspective. Opinion stories are disproportionately represented at the top of news sites' most-shared lists. Internal Facebook memos made public in the fall of 2021 revealed that the company had been rewarding outside content that users reacted to with the "angry face" emoji with better placement in news feeds. Within this context, ESPN's management selects and hammers characters and storylines that it believes will be especially divisive: Tim Tebow, LeBron James and whether or not he chokes or is better than Michael Jordan, the Dallas Cowboys in general, and so on. "I was told specifically, 'You can't talk enough Tebow,'" pundit Doug Gottlieb said after leaving the network.

At some time in roughly 2017, Jim Harbaugh and his purported overratedness became one of ESPN's choice subjects. Stephen A. Smith doesn't actually talk much about college football, although there have been at least five *First Take* segments about whether Harbaugh will leave Michigan for the NFL. (He hasn't—and as of this writing, it seems like he won't, but he almost did, and we'll come back to this later.) But ESPN has a takes guy specifically for the sport: Paul Finebaum, a longtime Birmingham, Alabama, radio host who has a TV show on the SEC Network (which ESPN owns) and appears frequently on the main channel. (Cowherd also started in radio, and you could say the country's hundreds of sports-talk stations might, in aggregate, rival ESPN's power to set narratives. Many of them, though, are ESPN affiliates that air network-produced shows, and there is a lot of stylistic overlap. The hot take dominates all mediums.)

Finebaum, sixty-six, is skinny and bald on top and wears glasses and nice suits that make him look like a lawyer. I assume that part of his hold on a large segment of his core audience is that they simultaneously respect and hate him for presenting himself as their social superior. In any case, between 2017 and 2019—again, before Michigan's poor 2020 season, when it was a top-ten program swimming, to some extent, against the tide of history—Finebaum really got on Harbaugh's ass. He referred to him, on Twitter and on TV appearances, as "the most overpaid coach in college football history," "a colossal failure," and "a total fraud." Finebaum said Harbaugh "looked like an idiot" after the 2018 Ohio State game and that he rooted for the Buckeyes to "humiliate" the Michigan coach every year in the rivalry matchup.

He—Finebaum—referred to Michigan's performance at one point in 2019 as "stunningly embarrassing" and said, "I could pick up the yellow pages of college coaches right now, close my eyes and pick a better coach than Jim Harbaugh."

It was a little much. There's something of the aspiring nationalist strongman in what Cowherd and Finebaum do—telling the people of Cowboys Nation or Hungary, as it were, that a primacy of strength and status is their birthright and that it has been lost because of the weakness and decadence of their quarterback, general manager, head coach, or Hungarian president.

There happens to be a useful control group in Penn State and its coach, James Franklin. Franklin got his job a year before Harbaugh at a program that has had a comparable level of success in the postintegration era. Since then, he has a winning percentage of .663 at PSU, whereas Harbaugh's at U of M is .718. Franklin is not an ESPN character. During the period described, as far as I can find, Finebaum tweeted about him once and did two TV segments about him. Finebaum did make Franklin into a storyline on air in the fall of 2021, but only to suggest that the University of Southern California should hire him as its next coach because he has done so well at Penn State.

Fine, you're now saying, *let's stipulate that the nasty media has been very unfair to Mr. Harbaugh. Who gives a shit?* It's another fair question. There are more urgent issues in the world, including but not limited to climate change. Also, Harbaugh did lose the games he lost; they didn't make that up. And on occasion, he knowingly goaded members of the press, like Paul Finebaum, who he referred to in a dismissive 2017 tweet as "Pete." Still, you got tired of his record being the only thing you ever heard about. Most of the people watching Michigan games are Michigan fans, yet they spoke to us every week like we had been in a coma for four to six years. With the guidance of a Tampa-based sports TV guru and archivist named Timothy Burke, I put together the transcripts of forty-three Michigan football broadcasts between 2018 and 2021.

There were at least thirty-one comments about Harbaugh not having beaten Ohio State in the file, and I didn't search the actual
games against Ohio State.

It was the only pitch they could throw, and the lack of any
other familiarity with what was going on was not an accident.
Thirty years ago, there were seven major conferences: SEC, Big
Ten, Big Eight, Southwest Conference, Pac-10, Big East, and ACC.
The biggest of those have steadily added more programs to maximize television ratings. The Pac-10 had to be renamed the Pac-12,
while the Big Eight and the Southwest formed the Big 12, which
currently has ten teams because two of them moved to the SEC. It
can't rename itself the Big Ten, though, because there's already a
Big Ten, which has fourteen teams in it.

Geography has been as strained as mathematics. Rutgers,
which is neither a good football program nor located in the Midwest, is now in the Big Ten because the Big Ten wanted its network to be carried in the New York City TV market; Oklahoma is
about to join the "Southeastern" Conference. The Big "East" no
longer exists as a football entity but at one point tried to add San
Diego State, as in the San Diego that is located on the Pacific
Ocean, next to Mexico. Teams no longer play regional rivals as
often, if at all, and are shuffled between channels and broadcast
teams in random ways to meet the needs of weekly TV schedules.
In the first six weeks of the 2018 season, Northwestern appeared
on ESPN, ESPNU, the Big Ten Network, Fox, Fox Sports 1, and
ABC—an example I'm using because when it made that year's Big
Ten championship game against Ohio State, Fox play-by-play man
Gus Johnson credited its first touchdown to Wisconsin.

In recent years, ESPN has reoriented its coverage around the
College Football Playoff, the four-team championship system,
launched in 2014, to which it has exclusive TV rights. When a
writer I know started working at the network in that year, new
employees at orientation were told that promoting the Playoff was
its top corporate priority. "They actually had little cards there that

ranked the company goals for 2014, with the Playoff number one," he told me. There are 130 top-level college football teams; only four or five of them have regularly made the Playoff. Nonetheless, according to an article that ran before the 2021 season in The Athletic, the network mentioned the Playoff twenty-seven times during one three-hour December 2020 episode of *College GameDay*. In the article, a producer for the network said it was going to try to stop humping the thing so much during the 2021 season; during the 2021 Cheez-It Bowl, which I watched as, uh, research for this book, there were nine Playoff promos and seven for other ESPN bowl games. One can only imagine how many there would have been if they hadn't cut back. In my file of Michigan broadcasts, the College Football Playoff, which the team did not participate in during the relevant period, was mentioned eighty-four times.

So the Graphic of Despair was an objective record of the team's performance but also a reminder of various tiresome provocations, of the seeming impossibility of doing any better, and of one's emotional attachments ultimately being commodities that are treated with varying degrees of intentional neglect and outright hostility for the benefit of the Disney corporation and Rupert Murdoch.

According to Karl Marx, in my understanding, alienation is the condition a person experiences when they have no autonomy over something personally or socially meaningful to them because it is subject to the power and incentives of accumulated capital. I believe I embody Marx's concept during each of the sixteen scheduled commercial breaks in college football games. On national broadcasts, these breaks are a minimum of two and a half minutes long and can last up to four minutes. Think about that. Five to eight full-length commercials in a row, often for the same three or four products, sixteen times a game. Broadcasts often take four hours. When YouTube users go rogue and post them online with all the superfluous breaks taken out—but with the game flowing at a normal pace, downtime between plays included—they can be more than two hours shorter.

What are you gonna do, though? You can't switch to another channel that has your game on. Fans aren't going to stop watching their teams, and conferences believe they have to get as much money as possible because otherwise another conference is going to get the money and use it to get better at football.

I spoke about the matter with John Kosner, a former executive vice president of ESPN who now runs his own sports media investment and advisory company. Kosner grew up in New York City and became a fan of college football because it was, in his words, "so different from anything I experienced." He recounted the stakes of a Thanksgiving 1971 game between Nebraska and Oklahoma that he remembered watching. "It had everything," he said. "It was everything you would imagine from middle of the country, a super-rivalry between states." (I think he is right that a football game between Oklahoma and Nebraska would have been the exact conceptual opposite of 1970s New York City.) "That game doesn't happen anymore because Nebraska chose to go to the Big Ten," he said wistfully.

Of course, as he recognized, the reason Nebraska chose to go to the Big Ten was because of the television money that was available to it in exchange for consolidating its brand with those of other national draws like Michigan, Ohio State, and Penn State. That money was offered to the school and its well-compensated administrators by executives like John Kosner. Did that make him feel a little bad? "You're making deals at the demand of these conferences and of the media companies you work for and it's a competitive arena," he said. "You might decide, 'Gee, this is terrible. We shouldn't do this.' But if you decide not to make a deal, someone else is going to make that deal.

"This is a different sport, but I vividly remember a colleague at ESPN complaining when we were carrying way too many regular season college basketball games and the quality wasn't there. And the solution he thought of was, 'Well, let's drop like fifty games.' So another colleague of mine wisely pointed out, 'Okay. So what's going to happen to those other fifty games?' And my friend said, 'Well, Fox will have them.' If Fox has them, then what have you really achieved?"

Sure, I said. But what about the goddang timeouts?

"What happens is the conference is saying, 'Okay, we want more for our rights, or we want $25 million for the Big 12 championship game,'" Kosner said. "And the answer frequently is, 'We want to expand the commercial for that.' And they say, 'Okay.'"

———————◆———————

Recruits responded to the Playoff by increasingly clustering at the schools that were initial competitors in the Playoff, giving those schools better chances of being selected for and winning subsequent Playoffs. When Elliott began calculating the blue-chip ratio in 2014, only one team had a number greater than 70 percent: Alabama, with 73 percent. Alabama is now up to 84 percent, with Georgia at 80 percent and Ohio State at 79 percent. While most players stay local, the best recruits are pursued nationally, a process that has also gotten easier for top schools because of digital film, which allows them to evaluate basically any player in the country. Elliott noted that Michigan's eminently decent performance according to advanced metrics was, to many such top players, basically irrelevant. "Recruits don't give a shit about power rankings. They'll look at the Playoff standings, they'll look at who's in the Playoff, they'll see who won the Ohio State-Michigan game, that type of stuff. They're not looking at SP+ or FPI or Sagarin or whatever metric you like," he said, naming some metrics I liked. "They want to see the name-brand win that you have." Recruits saw the Hated Self-Reinforcing Graphic of Despair too—that's one of the reasons it was self-reinforcing!

People inside the program were also conscious, perhaps too conscious, of what was being said outside of it. When I talked to

Chris Partridge, the former Michigan coach, I presented one or two theories I had about why the team hadn't won its biggest games when he was there. He said he had tried to come up with such an explanation himself—"it drove me crazy"—but in hindsight felt there wasn't much more to the matter than bad luck. Then we had a conversation about two losses to Ohio State. The first one took place in 2016 in Columbus, when the Buckeyes' quarterback was quite obviously stopped short on a fourth and one run that would have ended the game, only for the biased and incompetent officiating crew to award a first down anyway. (Ohio State fans have a different perspective on this event—the wrong perspective.) The second was in 2018, when Ohio State would have suffered a deflating upset and been eliminated from the Big Ten race the week prior if University of Maryland's quarterback hadn't missed a short two-point conversion throw to a wide-open receiver in the end zone in overtime. My conversation with Partridge, ostensibly an interview between a professional journalist and an expert, could have easily been between me and any other addled superfan. Here is the Rev.com transcription service's version of the exchange:

Ben Mathis-Lilley: They've had some bad luck in a couple games. In that 2016 game, and—

Chris Partridge: Just think about if we would have beat Ohio State in that game. It's a whole different direction. Think about 2018 when Maryland is about to beat Ohio State. They short hop the ball in the end zone. If they would have won that game, we would have won the Big Ten.

BML: Mm-hmm (affirmative). Mm-hmm (affirmative).

CP: But instead, Ohio State wins, we play them the next week, and they beat us. If Maryland beat them at that point, we're the Big Ten East champions, and we get a whole different Ohio State team the next week.

BML: Mm-hmm (affirmative). Mm-hmm (affirmative).

CP: So those little things in football, that can make the difference.
Those are the things that make the difference in what happens
and the confidence of a program.

"Mm-hmm (affirmative)" indeed. I spent Wisconsin week fearing
a cascade of little things going wrong. It was a road game, and
while Wisconsin was not as good as it had been in most recent seasons, it was still a decent team that would finish the season 9-4 and
was favored by Las Vegas by two points. The matchup had the vin-
tage notes and mouthfeel of a game in which Michigan would be
competitive until one of its players made an unlikely or unlucky
mistake in a crucial situation, giving Wisconsin a drive on which
it had a chance to seal the game. Then one of its players would do
something clutch and unlikely in an equally crucial situation, and
the Badgers would ultimately win by, let's say, eleven points. It had
that feeling. It was going to go to show once again that Jim Harbaugh something something Michigan big games something
something, and I was going to barf and light myself on fire.

As defensive lineman Mike Morris said after the team crushed
Northern Illinois, "We know if we lose a game, everyone's gonna
say, 'Oh, Michigan sucks again.'"

The Badgers were also a troubling opponent symbolically,
because for the last two decades or so, Wisconsin had been exem-
plifying Michigan's virtues better than Michigan. A series of head
coaches who'd each worked for one of their predecessors had built a
winning operation with an uncanny ability to identify beefy
young men who had neck tendons the size of elevator cables but
also possessed the insane world-class lateral quickness required to
end up as NFL offensive linemen or defensive ends or linebackers.
To wit, soon-to-be Hall of Fame offensive tackle Joe Thomas,
drafted out of Wisconsin in 2007, attended Brookfield High School
in Wisconsin's Waukesha County, while future Hall of Fame

defensive end J. J. Watt, drafted out of Wisconsin in 2011, attended Pewaukee High School, which is also in Waukesha County, nine miles away. (As did his younger brother, T. J. Watt, who shares the all-time NFL single-season sack record.) In 2020, the Dallas Cowboys drafted Wisconsin center Tyler Biadasz, who is from Amherst, Wisconsin (population 1,039) to replace retiring former Wisconsin center Travis Frederick, who is from Walworth, Wisconsin (population 2,821). What the hell?

Whatever sort of dairy witchcraft was going on in Waukesha County, the beef boys had rolled the beef train over Michigan in most of the teams' recent matchups, including 2019 (359 rushing yards for Wisconsin) and 2020 (341 rushing yards). Wisconsin was an excellent Midwestern university that had found its football niche (continuity of the beef process) and consistently won a lot of games. It probably wasn't going to win the national championship, but it had calibrated its expectations and goals very well relative to its resources. Meanwhile, here was Michigan going from one thing to another, still trying to be a national powerhouse, and constantly tripping over its own ass and falling into a well with a beehive stuck on its head. Shit. Should we *aspire* to be Wisconsin?

I had also made an unconscionable mistake regarding the weekend of the game, promising my son, who had recently turned five and loves fire trucks and firefighters, that we could drive to a parade that is put on annually by volunteer fire companies in the rural, mountainous part of New Jersey, which, I was as surprised as anyone to find out, is an actual existing part of New Jersey. It was a huge error, putting my family ahead of college football, and the parade started a half hour after the game. So we all drove the hour up there—I, my wife, and the three kids (there's also a three-year-old daughter and a nine-month-old baby)—and, at my insistence, watched the first quarter at a fortuitously excellent and accommodating Greek restaurant and bar that happened to be on the parade route.

The results were suspiciously promising. Wisconsin's defense was extremely tough and knew what it was doing; its line wasn't as easily pushed around, and its linebackers weren't as easily tricked into going the wrong direction, as the previous opponents' had been. There was always someone to smash into Haskins and Corum after they'd gone two or three yards. But they were getting those two or three yards. ("That is a tough dude," Harbaugh said of Corum later. "Some of the hits he took would have killed a lesser man.") And those yards were keeping Michigan's offense afloat long enough to occasionally get Wisconsin's goat with long passes. The one I saw before the parade started was a flea-flicker, where the running back takes the ball but then tosses it back to the quarterback for a long heave past the members of the defensive secondary, who are, hopefully, all like, "What? but I thought it was a running play!" When it happens, you have to say, "Flea-flicker!" out loud, which I did while standing with a beer in my hand next to a high table and kind of trying to watch my kids out of the corner of my eye. And when McNamara released the subsequent heave, it was in rhythm, with the confidence of someone who had an open receiver, and even though I couldn't yet see the receiver on the screen, I felt good about it and said, "Touchdown," which is what you do if you think there's going to be a touchdown, to show that you know how the game works. Indeed, wide receiver Cornelius Johnson was open, and he caught it for a thirty-four-yard touchdown. My wife wasn't watching. "I think we ordered too much food," she said.

When it had the ball, Wisconsin wasn't able to run on Michigan this time. Mike MacDonald, the new defensive coordinator, had changed Michigan's defensive scheme to involve larger linemen. He often put one more defensive tackle on the field than the previous coordinator had put on the field, which is the kind of absolutely, idiotically basic idea that fans often have about how to fix something. You know: We're getting pushed around out there!

We should have bigger guys! Why don't the coaches play the big-ger guys? Appallingly, it worked perfectly. Wisconsin recorded forty-three rushing yards on the day. Come on!

The parade started. Somehow, everything was functioning on my phone except ESPN, Twitter, and the web browser—a sick, disgusting joke, worse than what happened to Sisyphus or the guy who had the water disappear beneath him when he tried to drink. My wife's phone worked fine, and she kept tormenting me on pur-pose by saying things like "They scored again!" without telling me who *they* were. I kept sneaking away to look in the front win-dow of the restaurant only for there to be commercials on. At one point I was able to determine that Michigan was winning 13-3, but then a few minutes later it was 13-10, and the shock of seeing that score load on the phone was one I wouldn't wish on my worst enemy (my wife). We were near the start of the parade route, and from our vantage point in the grass along the two-lane state road it was proceeding down, we could see, to our left, a line going up the mountain (?!) where the subsequent companies and local marching bands and such were mustering. Despair-inducingly, they never stopped doing so; there would be a break, and I would think, *I'll be able to catch the fourth quarter,* and then Yankee Fucking Doodle and the goddamn Pequannock Township Fife and Drum Corps or whatever would turn a corner moving about one and a half miles per hour.

My son and daughter had a fantastic time. (The baby is always having a fantastic time.) The weather was perfect, and the fire-fighters and everyone around us were very nice. People would walk by and smile, the trucks would honk at the kids, and the people in the trucks would wave. There were different sizes and colors and styles of trucks, and they had different kinds of lights and sirens. When we got back in the car to go home, Michigan was ahead 23-10, then it was 31-10, and by the time we arrived, they had won 38-17.

An unexpected thing happened at the end of the third quarter. At Wisconsin home games, that is when the PA system plays the '90s rap standard "Jump Around" and the fans in the stadium, particularly the students, shout and jump up and down in unison and shake the massive concrete structure beneath them. It's one of the opposing-team traditions you can't help but respect. But on this day, in a city where their team hadn't won a game since 2001, the Michigan players also leaped to their feet to dance when the song came on. It was a sudden and coordinated attack, which junior safety Dax Hill referred to afterward as a plan to "steal" Wisconsin's "juice." Fox's announcing team was genuinely taken aback by the ferocity of Michigan's energy. On the videos posted on YouTube by fans who were there, most of the stadium is a sea of slowly waving red, but at its center there is a cluster of a hundred-odd Michigan players and staffers wearing white on the visiting sideline, vibrating much faster and more actively than anyone else, like an invasive biological force. Jumping, waving towels, screaming, gesturing to the crowd, but happily rather than in the frowny tough-guy way you typically see in sports. What a terrible thing it must be, to have your juice stolen.

The 2020 season, as bad as it had been, appeared to have functioned like a fire break, cutting off the program from the burdens of its recent past. There was a group of older players, highlighted by Hutchinson and Haskins, who played like they were furious, just boiling over, that their careers had not gone as they'd hoped. There were even more young guys like Corum, both quarterbacks, several of the offensive linemen, and a preposterously athletic defensive end named David Ojabo—who'd moved from Nigeria to Scotland at age seven and then gotten sent to New Jersey at age seventeen to play high school basketball, only to get pulled into football because he was so strong and fast—who were too inexperienced and foolish to think they couldn't do it. Why not them? What if they just won all the big road games, huh?

The most important sequence of the second half, on the actual field, happened during the third quarter, after Michigan had advanced the ball to Wisconsin's ten-yard line for a first and goal. Corum ran twice, moving the line of scrimmage forward to the three. Then Haskins took a handoff and was hit hard at the line of scrimmage but spun away and fell close to the goal line. Fourth and goal, from about three inches away. McCarthy, the freshman, was in the game. (It's rare for teams to play two quarterbacks, but McCarthy, a coveted five-star recruit who is much faster than McNamara, was getting to play a few times each game, mostly to run the ball or fake a run while handing off.) He took the snap and dove into the pile. Haskins slammed into him from behind to push him forward, which is, amusingly, legal. Mike Sainristil, an undersized wide receiver from Massachusetts who was born in Haiti and, according to his official MGoBlue.com profile, sings in the choir at his church, joined the desperate mass as well. McCarthy slid to his right and forward. It was a touchdown. Ten yards through the heart of farm country on four tough runs, and the game was essentially over.

The next week's matchup was against Nebraska. Nebraska had done a reverse Wisconsin. They had been really good for a long time and couldn't let go of that history, which had made them much worse. In 2003, their athletic director fired a coach named Frank Solich who'd won three-quarters of his games, giving a press conference at which he announced that "anyone who doesn't want to win the national championship shouldn't bother applying for this job." Said the AD, "I refuse to let the program gravitate into mediocrity." The next coach was fired after four years with a winning percentage just above .500, the definition of mediocrity. I'd actually forgotten this had happened with Solich because Nebraska recently did the same thing again, firing a recurring college football character named Bo Pelini—who had never won fewer than nine games in seven years as the Cornhuskers' coach but had never won more than ten—only for Pelini's successor to get canned after three years in which he went exactly 19-19. The next coach after that, Scott Frost, was supposed to be good, having previously led the University of Central Florida to an undefeated season, but had also been bad.

The Huskers had gotten a raw deal from the whole changing face of America thing. When I was interviewing the demographer, Ken Johnson, it had become clear that he didn't follow college football too closely, which made the aside he fired at the state even more devastating:

> Well, population decline, or slow growth, is much more common in rural areas and has been for most of the last century. It's more common in agricultural areas, rural farm areas, like down the Great Plains, for example. It is more typical in white areas, areas that are remote from metropolitan areas. I mean, as you know, there're some parts of the United States where they don't even have enough children or young boys in school to play full eleven-person football teams, as I understand it. So that would be another factor. I don't know the extent to which Michigan recruited from those areas, but certainly I could—I mean, if you were talking about places like Nebraska, or something like that, I could see where they literally might have a smaller pool to draw from.

The game, at night in Lincoln, actually went something like I had expected the Wisconsin game to go. Michigan was the better team on what those of us who are savvy viewers like to refer to as a "down to down basis," typically winning the push at the line of scrimmage. But in the second half, Frost, a pale, large-shouldered former Nebraska quarterback who, in my opinion, is kind of a smart aleck with one of those faces that makes you think, "I'd like to see this smart aleck get what he deserves," kept calling infuriating circus plays, where everyone would go one direction except one guy, who would leak out the other way surreptitiously and then receive a ridiculous looping moonball pass that dropped inches past the fingers of the panicked Michigan linebacker or defensive back trying to recover. Nebraska led by three going into the fourth quarter.

That was when it was Cade McNamara time, in a kind of funny and limited sense of it being a college quarterback's time in a big game on national TV. McNamara is a contradiction of personality and playing style. He's from Reno, Nevada, and is handsome in a football guy way. (He has appeared in an ad for Tom Brady's clothing line.) His head is kind of shaped like a cinder block, and he sometimes has frosted blond tips on his hair. He once praised his younger brother in an Instagram post for having played a whole high school season with a broken collarbone. None of it screams *cerebral*. But on the field, he acts like he has a football computer in his brain. He almost never throws interceptions, and he also almost always throws the ball within three seconds of the snap, which means he's almost never sacked. He throws a lot of short passes. He gets the ball to Michigan's running backs in the right spots, which is harder than it looks, given the different shifts and misdirection and stuff that the playbook includes. It's mostly not highlight material, but he knows the right place to put the ball, and he puts it there, and then at the end of the game, hey, wow, it looks like Michigan won again. After years of quarterbacks not even being able to get snaps off in time, or running around dynamically and then throwing the ball to the wrong team, McNamara just did what the situation called for.

Although Sam Webb had been suggesting that McCarthy should get more playing time and a 247Sports "insider" named "Dotman" had written that Harbaugh was allegedly considering putting him in earlier in the game than usual, it was McNamara who saved the team against Nebraska. Without completing a pass longer than fourteen yards, he supervised two long scoring drives to keep Michigan in the game after Nebraska touchdowns. Finally, safety Brad Hawkins, another guy who'd been on the team forever, ripped the ball away from Nebraska's quarterback, Adrian Martinez, with a minute and forty-five seconds left and the game tied. It was another of the plays in the season in which a Michigan veteran seemed to express what one of my peers in the writing field, Herman Melville, described as "the sum of all the general rage and hate felt by his whole race from Adam down." (He meant the human race, I believe.) Martinez had gained a first down and was trying to keep his legs moving to push the pile forward. Hawkins approached from his position in the defensive backfield, grabbed the ball, and pulled the hell out of it until Martinez fumbled. Goddang it, Hawkins's body language said. Not this time. Michigan kicked a field goal and won the game. The TV cameras captured Harbaugh and Hutchinson screaming into each other's faces as time ran out.

Put that on your damn graphic! Michigan was 6-0. Maybe there didn't need to be any settling for Wisconsin status. All they had to do now to vanquish the haters was beat Michigan State in East Lansing at the end of the month. And even though Michigan State was undefeated, they didn't really seem that good, so that was probably going to be easy.

INTERLUDE

Jim Harbaugh, explaining on the Monday after Michigan's victory over Nebraska why he had called the game a "Clint Eastwood win" shortly after it ended:

That's a great question. There's so many Clint Eastwood things, whether it was *El Camino* or *Dirty Harry* or *Unforgiven*, just some different things. Suffice it to say, "Make my day. Go ahead, make my day." There's some other ones that I'll just keep in my own mind.

CHAPTER

7

LSU vs. Florida

Ben Mathis-Lilley: Is there a faction that sometimes says, "Look, we take football seriously here, but are we taking it too seriously?" Are there internal critics of that—of the level of importance it has around the school?

Ross Dellenger: No.

I PLANNED TO VISIT Baton Rouge for a Louisiana State game because Ed Orgeron was the best possible proof that being extremely identifiable as a native of a given place helped make you a good football coach there. He and his team were to have an important place in this book as a thriving contrast to the mediocrity that was expected at Michigan. LSU was going to demonstrate that a program could be very successful even as it attempted to suppress the contradictions inherent in a supposedly amateur and education-related sport being played for free, mostly by Black athletes, for the financial benefit of white administrators (and the entertainment of white fans who did not hold the ideals of higher education in high regard). Moreover, I was going to have a raging time at epic tailgates before seeing a high-stakes night game with 102,000 largely shirtless Tiger freaks.

Well, Orgeron and LSU's football team screwed that all up.

In a GIF from the sitcom *Community* that circulates online, the character played by actor Donald Glover is returning with several boxes of pizza to what he thinks is an ongoing party. When he opens the door, however, the floor is covered in broken glass, the room is on fire, someone is running past the camera swinging a flaming shirt over his head, and someone else appears to be dead. This was basically the scene in Louisiana when I arrived in October, with the team having already lost three games, including one the previous week against Kentucky.

The first thing I noticed *was* fire, while driving northwest away from the New Orleans airport late at night, although it was a fire that was supposed to be there—the so-called flare above the Valero company's St. Charles oil refinery. (The flare, I have now learned, burns off unusable gases that are the result of making the products that get sold.) After passing the refinery and a casino that shared its building with a gas station, I drove to Baton Rouge and straight to the original Raising Cane's chicken fingers drive-through, where there were nine cars ahead of me at 12:18 a.m.

These were the Louisiana values I had heard so much about. Earlier in the week, I had sent a message to three local contacts asking what I should do in the free time I had before the game. Within fourteen minutes, they had sent twelve restaurant recommendations and a picture of some gumbo that one of them was already cooking for the weekend. The only other recommendation was to "go see where Huey got shot."

I was going to do that the next morning, but for now I was staring at Ed Orgeron. Not the actual Ed Orgeron, head coach, but a large image of his face on my fountain soda. There was also one on the takeout bag. It said "Geaux Eaux" underneath his face. Someone in Cane's corporate had probably already ordered new bags. "I'm not telling you anything you don't know," a booster named John Hawie would tell me the day before the game. "He's done."

It had been a swift rise and fall for Orgeron. In fact it had been many swift rises and falls. He was raised in the small south Louisiana town of Larose, which is on the part of the map below New Orleans that seems to dissolve into the Gulf of Mexico. Orgeron earned a scholarship to play football at LSU in 1979 but dropped out. He got another chance to play at a school called Northwestern State in Natchitoches, Louisiana, but was nearly removed from the team when an administrator accused him and his roommate of breaking all the furniture in their dorm room. (The roommate denies it; Orgeron does not appear to have spoken about the allegation on the record.) After college he got into the football business and rose to become the defensive line coach for the dominant University of Miami program of the late '80s and early '90s, but he was dismissed from the job after a Florida woman obtained a restraining order against him and he was arrested for head-butting the manager of a bar in Louisiana. (He reportedly completed a domestic violence program related to the restraining order, and charges were dropped in the bar case.) After rehabbing his career at lower-tier schools and, he says, getting sober, he again became the line coach for a top program, this time USC under Pete Carroll. In 2004, Ole Miss hired him as its head coach.

According to an account by college football writer Steven Godfrey, one of the first things Orgeron did at Ole Miss was take off his shirt in a meeting and challenge the team's players to fight him, in order to make some sort of point about toughness. According to another college football writer, Andy Staples, Orgeron told every-one at practice, *including members of the staff,* to try to recover fumbled balls, resulting in an assistant coach dislocating his shoulder. He conducted a full-contact scrimmage amid a weather delay during an actual game, which Ole Miss lost by twenty-four points when it resumed. He also apparently would walk through the halls of the football building early in the morning whaling on a marching band bass drum. In three years, he went 3-21 in con-ference play and got fired.

Then he went back to USC for an assistant job, where he was said to have learned and mellowed out—yes, again—and from there to LSU, getting the head gig after Les Miles (the guy who ate the grass and won the 2007 national championship) was fired because he had reliably started to lose three or more games each season. Shortly after Orgeron's hiring was announced, fourteen hundred people came to a banquet in his honor in Larose, including Edwin Edwards, the longtime state politician whose Wikipedia page includes two distinct sections on indictments that are themselves distinct from the section called "Early Scandals." Edwards is both the person who made the quip about not losing a race unless he was "caught in bed with either a dead girl or a live boy" and the one who successfully ran against David Duke in a campaign remembered for the bumper-sticker slogan "Vote for the crook, it's important." (Edwards's campaign did not create the bumper sticker.)

Given his background, it was not surprising when Orgeron's tenure started off erratically, with excellent recruiting and some big wins but also gear-grinding losses where the offense looked concerningly bad. It was somewhere from a little to incredibly sur-prising when, in 2019, he helmed what may have been the best college football team of all time and was at least the most dra-matically triumphant. Led by a transfer quarterback from Appa-lachia (Joe Burrow), two wide receivers who would become NFL stars as rookies (Justin Jefferson and Ja'Marr Chase), and an ungodly number of other elite talents (five, including Burrow and Jefferson, were selected in the first round alone of the next NFL draft), the team went 15-0, vanquished Nick Saban's Alabama machine in Tuscaloosa in a 46-41 classic, and beat Clemson for the national championship in a game that had long been scheduled, as if fated by the spirits of the shrimp boats, to be played in the Superdome in New Orleans. Burrow, who had transferred away from Ohio State after three seasons in which he rarely appeared on the field, won the Heisman Trophy. Accepting the award, he became emotional while thanking Orgeron for giving him the chance to play. "He just means so much to me and my family," the quarterback said of the coach. "I sure hope they give him a lifetime contract. He deserves it."

But before the 2020 season, the assistant who'd been responsible for LSU's record-setting passing offense left for the NFL, and the team's defensive coordinator became Baylor University's head coach. LSU then went 5-5, looking discombobulated in all facets. The replacement defensive coordinator, recurring college football character Bo Pelini, was shitcanned; the offensive coordinator retired; and Orgeron was suddenly on the spot. Many expected that he'd be up to the job—the Vegas over/under line for 2021 was 8.5 wins, which meant eight or nine wins were considered the most likely outcomes. Posters on the infamous Tiger Rant message board were mostly predicting ten wins or more, as were some beat writers and sensible national pundits like Staples.

The reasoning went that there were too many good players on LSU for it to lose more than a few games. Orgeron, as one might surmise from the many second chances that have been offered to him, is a guy whom people want to like in spite of their better judgment. (Hawie told me Orgeron's good-old-boy persona conceals interpersonal savvy. "He can read people extraordinarily well," he said.) His area of specialty at USC had been recruiting, and his 2021 LSU team was fifth in the country in blue-chip ratio.

The 2021 season, though, had been a mess. LSU had played four major-conference opponents and lost to three of them, winning only against Mississippi State, which is not even the best team in Mississippi, a state that has a rich tradition of losing football. Kentucky had beaten LSU badly the previous week at a stadium called Kroger Field, at one point leading the game 35-7. Taken down to Chinatown by a basketball school at a field named for a grocery store. Embarrassing.

The next morning I took my acquaintance's advice and went to see where Huey got shot. That would be Huey "the Kingfish" Long, who was the governor of the state from 1928 until 1932 and then one of its US senators in such a way that, as I understand it, he was basically still the governor at the same time. Long campaigned on the idea of taking money from the rich—oil companies, banks, and railroads—and giving it to the poor. He followed through on that promise to some extent upon taking office, but he also took from the rich to give to himself and the network of elected officials and government employees who helped him hold power.

LSU was launched as a military academy in 1860 under the direction of William Tecumseh Sherman, whose relationship with the South and its troops is mostly remembered today for other reasons. It was still fairly small when Long came to power but had begun building its modern-day campus. Like leaders elsewhere, Long viewed the state university and its football team as a useful means to an end, although he also seems to have really enjoyed watching football. From a 1939 *Time* magazine article: "Huey began to spend $13,500,000 on L.S.U. for sumptuous buildings, a monster swimming pool, 'professional' footballers, a huge Medical Center in New Orleans. Contractors, politicians and public jobsters fattened, and the student body jumped from 2,100 to 8,550. Midway in this adventure into education, Huey announced: 'If there's any title I'm proud of, it's Chief Thief for L.S.U.'"

At LSU, spectacle was always part of the sell. The marching band—the Golden Band from Tigerland—increased in size from 37 members to 150 during Long's time running the state, and he personally hired two of its directors. He wanted the band to make as many trips as possible with the team and is reputed to have personally leaned on the Illinois Central railroad until it reduced its fare for students so they could travel to a game against Vanderbilt. He doubled the size of the football stadium by building bleachers with dorms underneath them in a ploy to access money that had been allocated for student housing. He also hired football coaches and annoyed one of them—Biff Jones—into quitting by attempting to give a halftime pep talk to the team during a game in 1934. The dispute was covered in the *New York Times.* "Jones was reported hunting ducks in the coastal marshes and could not be reached for a statement," the article said about Biff.

Long told reporters "one of the topnotchers of the country" was being sought as Jones's replacement. Unfortunately, the Kingfish was not present to see the team win its first SEC championship under successor Bernie Moore in 1935 because in September of that year, he got shot and died. This was what I had arrived at the state capitol building to learn about. The building is a thirty-four-story Art Deco skyscraper, the tallest state capitol in the country, that was planned and built under Long. It stands alone past the north end of downtown, fronted by a large lawn and abutted to the back and side by a lake and a smallish park. Its exterior is adorned with various classical sculptural details (state symbols like pelicans, emblems of law and science, etc.), and it has a 120-foot-long entrance hall with 37-foot ceilings in which every surface is either covered by an ornate custom mural or made out of marble, bronze, or gold. It is pretty cool, and you can just walk around it doing whatever, which is a refreshing feeling in these times. The legislature was not in session, and I was basically the only person there except for some staff. I took an elevator to a

twenty-seventh-floor observation deck, where the view is dominated by an ExxonMobil refinery to the north.

Back on the ground floor, a sixtysomething docent showed me
holes in the marble walls near an elevator bank that may or may
not have been from the bullets that Long's bodyguards fired at a
doctor named Carl Weiss during the encounter in which Long was
shot. Authorities immediately identified Weiss as Long's killer, but
the investigation was not extensive, and there are a lot of open
questions. Weiss's motive was not clear, though he might have
been angry at Long about a patronage-related political move that
had affected his father-in-law. He might have shot the senator, or
punched him, or just confronted him and startled Long's bodyguards because he was armed (doctors who carried drugs sometimes also carried a gun). It's not clear whether Weiss or a
panicking bodyguard fired the bullet that killed Long. Regardless, Long definitely got hit, dying just over a day later, and Weiss
died right in the capitol, having been shot, a later study would conclude, about two dozen times. (A tough break for him if he had
really just wanted to talk.) The docent told me her husband had
played football for Paul Dietzel, the LSU coach who had won the
team's last national championship of the twentieth century in
1958. She too believed Orgeron was as dead, metaphorically, as Dr.
Carl Weiss had been after being shot twenty-four times. She said
the next coach needed to be a "disciplinarian."

On the one hand, it was true that Orgeron had lost three games
already and that the team looked bad. On the other hand, he was
one and a half seasons removed from coaching the greatest team
ever. Jim Harbaugh had been retained despite going .500 over the
course of two years, and he had never gone 15-0 before that. So it
was with an eye toward understanding the differing standards at
work that I went to visit Hawie, an LSU athletics donor who lives
in Baton Rouge.

I was intrigued by the chance to meet a southern football
booster in person. There isn't really a position like it in professional

sports. There is no specific barrier to entry, but the club is exclusive: people with enough enthusiasm for their team, and enough money to spend, that they are essentially part of management.

This booster lived in a neighborhood of newly built homes a short drive from the city center. His house was nice and airy but not enormous or extravagant, although there was a turquoise 1957 Chevy Bel Air convertible in the three-car garage. The walls of his second-floor den were covered floor to ceiling in framed game programs dating back to the Long era. (One of the covers, from 1935, is a full-page ad for cigarettes.) He owns about eight hundred of them.

Hawie is on the shorter side and in his midfifties, and he was wearing a tucked-in polo shirt. He has evidently been successful in a career managing investments. He's not Louisianan or even an alum, but he spent part of his childhood in Atlanta and became a Tiger fan by listening to the team at night on the radio. LSU games have been broadcast for decades on WLL, a clear-channel AM station in New Orleans, and many of them are scheduled in the evening, a tradition that began in the 1930s. (Clear-channel stations are so called because they are powerful enough to send their signal over entire regions of the country, and the FCC keeps their frequency clear across those regions for that purpose.) The school's version of the story is it wanted to play games in cooler temperatures and enable day-shift refinery workers to attend. A writer and southern football expert named C. J. Schexnayder, however, pointed me to a 1968 book in which the athletic director who originated the practice said he'd done so because "we had many well-to-do fans whose duties running nearby plantations made it impossible to get away on a Saturday afternoon."

It was the mystique that captured Hawie's interest, the roars from LSU's "Death Valley" stadium beamed through the dark skies of the South, rather than consistent team success. In the first three and a half decades of his life, LSU won only three conference titles and didn't win a national championship. He attended games as often as possible, though, and even flew to Baton Rouge for that purpose while working in Luxembourg, becoming well-known as the guy who flew from Luxembourg to Louisiana for games. He joined the board of the Tiger Athletic Foundation (TAF), the entity that funds LSU sports, at around the turn of the century, when college football's most recent wave of fundraising and spending escalation was beginning to build. Pro teams had realized the revenue-generating possibilities of adding luxury boxes, suites, and lounges to their stadiums, and college teams were following the trend. Hawie says the expenses for his twenty-five-seat suite add up to about $100,000 a year, a cost he splits with three other people. (He no longer commutes from Luxembourg, having worked in Baton Rouge since 2009.)

When Hawie joined TAF, LSU was expanding its stadium by issuing bonds; he says he was brought on because of his experience in finance. LSU's coach was the now-vaunted Nick Saban, who had been hired in 1999 after a moderately successful run at Michigan State. At LSU, Saban was paid about $1.5 million a year, a salary considered so high at the time that the AP ran a story about it; even adjusted for inflation, that would be something like the fortieth-highest salary in the game today, and less than half of what Orgeron was making.

Saban has been so successful at Alabama, and was so successful before that at LSU, that he is thought of as an omniscient, sinister figure. A few people I spoke to mentioned that one key to his success is that he manages donors with an iron hand. He's also one of the coaches whose teams are widely assumed to be paying players a lot of money under the table—a person who's been around high school and college football for decades told me that Saban was a leader in that aspect of the "recruiting" process, and for what it's worth, a witness named Marty Blazer, in a federal trial related to college sports finances, testified that Alabama football players were among those to whom he'd made payments. (Saban has denied that Alabama ever violated any rules against paying players.)

Hawie seemed like a fairly frank person, so I asked him what Saban did behind the scenes, hoping to hear more about what *Sports Illustrated*'s Richard Johnson had called his "Look, mother-fuckers, we're going to do it this way" style. Said Hawie, "He came to the TAF board and said, 'I need three things. I need the football facility separate from the athletic department,'" as in, physically separate, standing alone. "'Secondly, I need a good letterman organization,'" as in the group that maintains relationships with former players. "And I think the third thing was he needed the academic center for athletes to be better staffed. And that's what they raised money for."

These are wildly boring things to be demanding of your southern money men in high-level meetings. They were not the goods that I sought, although Hawie did also mention that he once saw another donor tell former athletic director Joe Aleva he would provide $4 million to buy out Miles's contract. But the demands were instructive about what has made Saban so successful: identifying and destroying impediments to winning. The football facility had to be custom designed so the players could practice and do conditioning with maximum efficiency, the former players needed to be in a good mood so that there wouldn't be bad press or factional disputes within the program, and the academic center had to be working at top capacity to eliminate distractions regarding eligibility. The idea was to surround the ostensibly amateur athletes with professionalism, chiseling away their lives and obligations until the only thing they had left to worry about was getting better at football. Hawie had played a small part in helping Saban take LSU football to this modern level.

The coach took an equally "look, motherfuckers" approach on the field, it seems. Longtime NFL safety Ryan Clark, who played for the Tigers when Saban arrived, told me that players were not initially inclined to listen to "some short guy" (Saban is five feet, six inches) with such apparently limitless self-regard. "Nick Saban wasn't *Nick Saban* when he got to LSU. He didn't have seven national championships then," Clark said. "So at the time, listening to him saying, you don't look like a football team, and you guys will do this and that, and this needs to change, and this is why you guys were bad—like, hold on, man. You're coming from Michigan State, you don't know nothing!" He paused briefly. "But it turned out he knew a lot."

Saban won the first of his seven national championships at LSU and set up his successor, Miles, very well. But he had left LSU for the NFL, then left the NFL and created LSU's modern nemesis at Alabama. Saban is from West Virginia but played college ball and spent his early career in Ohio, and he has been itinerant since; he doesn't register as being from any particular place. Orgeron, who is built like a henchman, wears his hair at military length, and parts it down the middle. He has a loud, deep, and abrasive speaking voice that is sometimes difficult for outsiders to understand. Hawie said that many of the people around the program had not let go of the idea that LSU deserved someone with Saban's air of sophistication and professionalism rather than a Cajun like Orgeron. "They're not going to go good old boy again," he said. "There's been underlying hate toward him since the day he was hired."

This was easy to confirm on Tiger Rant, where I had found descriptions of Orgeron as a meathead, "a kiss-ass redneck hick," "a horrid face for the program, university and state," "a cartoon character that nobody takes seriously," and the coaching equivalent of Karl from *Sling Blade*, a 1996 movie about a mentally disabled backwoods man played by Billy Bob Thornton who kills three people. When a coach is on the hot seat, apocryphal stories about aberrant behavior and explosive behind-the-scenes conflict tend to circulate, and the dubious but appropriately déclassé anecdote that was aired on a local podcast about Orgeron was that he'd tracked down and challenged a group of people to a fight at their "fishing camp" in south Louisiana because one of them had made a critical comment about his coaching earlier in the day. "Someone recorded this interaction and sent it into the LSU administration," the host claimed, but the tape has not surfaced. I filed a Freedom of Information Act request with LSU for outside correspondence it had received regarding Orgeron, including potential documentation of misconduct, but its response did not include any such recordings.

One thing that verifiably happened was that someone had called Orgeron's radio show (broadcast weekly from an outlet of the local TJ Ribs restaurant chain) in early October 2021 and asked him to wish the caller's sister a happy birthday, which Orgeron did. Then the caller sarcastically cautioned Orgeron against having sex with her—seemingly a reference to a photo that had circulated online of the coach lying in bed with a young woman not long after he announced, in April 2020, that he was getting divorced. After a few seconds of muttering, Orgeron told the show's host that "down the bayou, we got a fishing hole for people like that." The highest paid public employee in the state was at TJ Ribs threatening to murder a radio caller for bringing up his sex accomplishments, although he was, you know, probably kidding. "He's literally one of us," a Tiger Rant poster wrote after this, finishing the thought with simple elegance: "We should never hire someone who is like us again."

I had stepped into the murky waters of southern football politics, in which a team must embody a distinct, purportedly more simple and old-fashioned culture while also proving that it can compete with and even surpass what is being done in the rest of the country. "Louisiana is down a lot of lists, but not football," LSU alum and radio host Charles Hanagriff told me. (There is a

Hanagriff's Machine Shop in the small south Louisiana community of Centerville. ("I'm the only one that didn't go into the family business," he said.)

Paul Putz, the Baylor historian, had given me some background. The idea of emulating a northeastern sporting ideal (or any northern ideal) was not super popular in the South in the late nineteenth century, he said, and many southern universities likewise precluded themselves from being considered among the nation's elite institutions, academically, by enforcing total segregation. (Michigan admitted Black students, although as late as the 1950s, according to one estimate, they made up only about 1 percent of the student population, and they were assigned only other Black students as dormitory roommates.) In the 1930s, southern teams were instrumental in normalizing the distribution of athletic scholarships and the playing of bowl games, because everyone else knew that the South was going to ignore rules against those things anyway. "I think the South really represents, more than anything else, a rejection of amateurism," Putz said. Victories over northern teams—Center College over Harvard in 1921 and Alabama over Washington in the 1926 Rose Bowl—became legendary.

Robert Mann was happy to talk to me about the lack of respect for the well-rounded academic ideal because it drove him nuts. Mann is a tall, trim individual who started his career in newspapers in northern Louisiana before spending several decades as a press secretary for the state's Democratic senators and governors, who are a dying breed. Now he is a professor of journalism at LSU. After the exchange that opens this chapter, *Sports Illustrated* college football writer and former LSU beat reporter Ross Dellenger had given me Mann's name. ("There *are* those critics, I guess, but they're not stopping anyone," he clarified, which was not intended as a shot at Mann and is probably something Mann would agree with.) I met him at the Barnes & Noble campus bookstore, where I attempted to order a pumpkin spice latte at the in-house Starbucks before being informed they were out of whatever pumpkin spice is made of, which was a humiliating experience.

Mann gave me a tour of campus and laid out the context that made Orgeron's termination seemingly imminent. For one, there were the bonds that had raised money for the stadium. There were ongoing payments on them, and the TAF had to make them. Its budget—remember, it finances the entire athletic department— is formally separate from the rest of the university. For a few years, it made an annual donation to the school's nonathletic oper- ations for appearances' sake, but athletic director Scott Woodward had announced he was ending that practice in 2019. "While I will always support the university in some form or fashion," he said, "we cannot sustain what we're currently doing." Two years later, LSU athletics could also not sustain the decline in football rev- enue that Orgeron's continued tenure portended. "They have bonds they have to pay off, and they're not guaranteed by the state," Mann said. "They can't just let it ride for a couple of years." LSU's endowment—the pool of donated money it essentially keeps as security and to generate income through investments— is about $500 million. That's thirty-four times smaller than Michigan's.

As Mann had suggested, the state was not ready to take up any slack. The governor from 2008 to 2016 was Bobby Jindal, a Repub- lican with presidential ambitions who sought to make his reputa- tion as a fiscal conservative by reducing public support for higher education in order to (among other things) make taxes on oil and gas companies even lower than they already were. Per Nola.com, the state funded 60 percent of the budgets for its system schools (including LSU) when Jindal took office. By the time he left, that number was down to 25 percent. The stunt was made all the more bleak in retrospect when Jindal's 2016 presidential campaign ended in November 2015, more than two months before primary voting even began, because he had no chance of winning or even contending.

Mann and I passed a building whose name had to be changed after the guy it was named for went to prison. Then we passed one named for Huey Long's successor and puppet governor, O. K. Allen. "He didn't do shit," Mann said. We were headed to the central library, which itself had been named for former LSU president Troy Middleton until a journalist named Asher Price found a letter Middleton had written in 1961 reassuring a correspondent that the school, though it had been forced to admit Black students, would make sure they didn't interact with whites. "We keep them in a given area," he wrote. The library is also in such bad shape that the bookshelves on its top floor have to be protected by a permanent system of tarps, funnels, and garbage cans because the roof leaks when it rains.

This has been an issue for years, although the photos I saw of the tarp setup were published alongside a recent story in the student newspaper, *Reveille*, which said the total estimated cost of all the deferred maintenance projects at LSU is $630 million. ("We've made the joke a lot of times that the next building that needs to be built on campus is the Shaquille O'Neal Memorial Natatorium and Central Library, because that's the only way we're going to get a new library built," an LSU sports blogger who goes by the pseudonym "PodKatt" told me, referring to the basketball program's most famous recent graduate.) Mann also showed me the building that houses the political science department, which he said didn't have handicapped access. The department is on its second floor, so if you can't climb stairs and you want to major in political science, administrators will have to arrange for your classes to be held elsewhere.

To me, the strangest thing about all of this was how unnecessary it seemed. LSU has a nice, expansive campus. The style is

"Italian renaissance," with red tile roofs and stucco walls. Its landscape is highlighted by the fairy-tale type of spacious oak trees whose lower branches are so close to the ground and big around that you can use them as benches. It's not at the top of the college ranking systems, but it's not at the bottom, and it has some respected academic programs. Baton Rouge has warm weather, and the food is so good that, while working my way through the restaurant recommendations I'd been given, I went to the hotel gym twice in one day to burn off calories so I could eat more of it.

The state has money too, in part because of its oil and gas resources; in 2020, Louisiana's GDP per capita was just below Vermont's and higher than Michigan's and Florida's. But the money is very unequally distributed—in the most recent census data, Louisiana has the highest poverty rate of any state besides Mississippi. Move a little bit of that money around, and, it seemed to me, you could have a destination town and university like the ones in, say, Austin or Columbus. People all over our great country are dying to move somewhere where the weather is warm, the living is good, and you can find housing that costs less than a trillion dollars a month.

The interest wasn't there, though. Although Bobby Jindal is not popular in Louisiana today, he won reelection to the governorship in 2011 by a forty-five-point margin. The condition of higher education, in a state with the fourth-lowest percentage of residents with a bachelor's degree in the United States, is not a superseding concern.

There is a 2016 book about related matters called *Strangers in Their Own Land* by sociologist Arlie Russell Hochschild, who spent several years making visits to the state. The people she spoke to do not consider themselves hostile to educational attainment and economic progress, per se. Instead, they see themselves as prioritizing other deserving values—self-sufficiency, for instance, and commitment to the traditions of family and community life in rural places and small towns.

The impulse to find a more presentable coach was also an insistence that being from Louisiana, and being from the country, didn't mean being backwards and dysfunctional. I heard multiple times that the next coach would be "clean." This was a reference to Orgeron's personal behavior but also to a series of investigative articles that began appearing in *USA Today* in November 2020 and were substantiated by an outside law firm's subsequent investigation. Both the newspaper and the firm found that LSU's Title IX office had failed to properly investigate or take action regarding a number of sexual assault complaints made against male students, including several football players. It was moreover revealed that Les Miles had been investigated internally in 2012 and 2013 for making advances on female students who worked for the football program—and that while he hadn't been fired, he had been instructed to stop contacting and being alone with student athletic department employees. (Miles denies that he ever behaved inappropriately, and LSU has said it takes its Title IX obligations seriously and is working to address shortcomings.) Mann was skeptical of the "clean" talking point. "They don't know what that means," he said. "They just mean someone who isn't going to get caught."

It was the night before the game. Still looking for ways to spend downtime that didn't involve food, I messaged a colleague who'd worked in Shreveport and covered LSU football in the past. He told me to "go to the zoo at the gas station in Grosse Tete." After some research, I found he was referring to a business called the Tiger Truck Stop about fifteen miles outside Baton Rouge. The Tiger Truck Stop had kept a tiger and a camel on its grounds, but it turned out the tiger had died in 2017, and in 2019, the camel had sat on a woman visiting from Florida who went into its enclosure to retrieve her dog, whose name was Baby Girl.

She told authorities and reporters she had bitten the camel's testicles to free herself. The gas station is now under new ownership, and the new owners got rid of the zoo component.

I drove around for a while instead, ending up on the west edge of town on the road that followed the levee along the Mississippi. I realized I'd never had a clear picture in my head of what a levee actually was. Here, at least, they are piles of earth fifty feet high that are covered in grass. They feel ancient, especially in the dark. The only lights in the sky were the blinking red radio towers farther out in the country and the white glow emitting from Tiger Stadium at the southwest corner of campus. Between the stadium and the river, RVs were rolling into gravel lots to park overnight for tailgating. I put Clifton Chenier, the king of Zydeco, on the car stereo and drove south. The road was a winding one, but it felt like heading straight into the past.

———◦|◦———

I'd seen Hanagriff the previous morning, when he was doing a radio show at a restaurant called Ruffino's. True to what I had come to think of as Louisiana form, it was in a nondescript ranch building on a haphazardly zoned state road, but when you stepped inside, you entered a different and better world: black-and-white tile, red carpet, dark wood, the kind of decor that organically generates Frank Sinatra songs. I wanted to move in and live there. Hanagriff was broadcasting from the bar with a cohost, a producer, and a representative of one of the show's advertisers, Supreme Rice. He was chatty between commercial breaks and had been kind to invite me, but the show was gambling focused, as more and more sports coverage is these days, which I find excruciatingly boring. Long conversations about things like what Colorado State's injury report might mean for its chances to score more than such and such number of points against New Mexico. Who cares? I talked to the Supreme Rice rep, who looked like a younger version of West Virginia senator Joe Manchin, a well-built guy with a haircut that you might call a power mullet.

Like everyone, he thought LSU was going to lose to Florida. "Max Johnson's gonna be good," he said about the starting quarterback. "But they don't have anyone blocking for him. And they can't run the ball for shit." I asked him where Orgeron had gone wrong. "He lost it when they were doing the social justice stuff and he didn't walk with 'em," he said.

That was something. I had seen this theory on Tiger Rant as well. In August 2020, Orgeron had appeared on Fox News and told a host, "I love President Trump." He had not previously been known for being politically opinionated, and he had actually appeared at a fundraiser for Democratic Louisiana governor John Bel Edwards. So maybe he was, in part, trying to be a normal, go-along-to-get-along authority figure. But Trump was not a normal president. George Floyd had been murdered by a police officer in Minnesota just a few months earlier, and Trump's administration had ordered the tear-gassing of a subsequent protest outside the White House. Two weeks after Orgeron's Fox appearance, a number of Black players marched from the football building to the university administration building. Orgeron—unlike coaches such as Saban at Alabama and Harbaugh at Michigan, who joined their players in similar protests—was not present until the players called and asked him to meet with them after the march.

That this was perceived as Orgeron's screw-up turned my head around given the attitudes that most white Louisianans, according to polling, hold about Black Lives Matter protests. ("Louisiana has a little more level of racial animosity or conservatism, I guess if you want to put it that way, racial conservatism," I had said in raising the issue with the pseudonymous PodKatt, who grew up in south Louisiana and lives about an hour from Baton Rouge. "You don't have to be delicate about it, man," he said. "It's definitely actual racism.") A similar tension existed between the southern power schools' established tradition of paying cash to Black athletes and the fact that polls consistently find that white Republicans are one of the demographic slices most opposed to paying college athletes.

I knew I was being naive about the motivations at work, but I could not figure out exactly how. A book called *The I in Team* by Emory University philosophy professor Erin Tarver proved valuable in this respect. Tarver is herself a Louisiana native and longtime LSU sports fan. She noticed at some point that the subjects of the high-minded critical and literary theory she was reading in academia—how societies end up getting organized like they do, beliefs about what it should mean to be a man or a woman, and so forth—were not unrelated to the conversations she was familiar with from sports. (The book begins with a reference to the male habit of asking women sports trivia questions to prove they are "real fans," which is definitely an insulting thing that other men, but not me, have done.)

Among the insights in her book, two seemed especially relevant to contemporary college football. One was that some fans don't think of players as embodiments of important values, as partners in a given community, but as possessions—as instruments, basically, who should feel fortunate for the chance that the fans and the institution have made available, an opportunity to be part of someone else's good thing. *Sports Illustrated*'s Johnson, a Florida native, summarized the idea like so: "It's an honor for them to come here. They should respect it and not step out of line after we gave them a scholarship. We gave them an opportunity to have a better life or get out of the inner city or yada yada yada, so those players owe their blood, sweat, tears, time, effort, and injuries to us because of what we bestowed upon them and how we helped them out."

(None of this condescension should necessarily be imputed to the gentleman from the rice company, who did not pass judgment

about the merits of the players' cause. But it's certainly the way
some fans feel about players at Louisiana State, Michigan, and
everywhere else.)

Another of Tarver's points was that disidentification with players and teams and their values is just as powerful a force, for many
fans, as identification. Complaining about the athlete or coach
who disgusts you is another way to announce what you think people *should* act like. Tarver amusingly centers this discussion
around the internet-generated concept of haterade, that is, the hater's beverage of choice. As she puts it memorably, "Haterade is, in
short, a crucial instrument in the production and reinforcement of
sports fans' identities." White LSU fans with certain views might
not think of the chance to complain about Black players' politics as
a reason they liked the team, per se. But Tiger Rant indicated that
it compelled and kept their attention.

Hanagriff didn't think much of these criticisms. "Everybody
that is involved is trying to make something better for themselves.
The players are trying to be better players, the coaches are trying
to move up the ladder, the fans are trying to enjoy it. And if we do
it right, it doesn't become an exercise in racial politics. Sports has
always been—well, I shouldn't say always has been, because in the
last couple years it's not. It was always the unifier, when I was
growing up."

Ryan Clark grew up across the Mississippi from downtown
New Orleans, started for LSU for three years, and had a long NFL
career that ended in 2014. He's now an ESPN analyst, and he
addressed George Floyd's death on the network before speaking at
another, larger march that LSU athletes held on campus in September 2020. Some Tiger Rant posters blamed this event in particular for the team's poor season. One accused Clark of making
players "believe they were victims," which was not my takeaway
from his speech. (A video of his remarks is available online.) Said
another, "He planted the seed, and the dissenters and head cases
around the program watered and fertilized it." (The idea that the

team had been destroyed by a single speech by a former player was met with some skepticism. "You idiots need to go outside and take a walk or something," one person said.)

In a way, Clark agreed with the white fans who felt that Orgeron's response to his players was a demonstration of incompetence, although he also thought it was a failure of empathy. "He wasn't smart enough to think, or humble enough to say, You know what? I better just do this so my boys feel supported. And that was probably my bigger problem than anything. Because it was like, damn, even knowing it would be the thing to make the boys feel like, You know what, he's here for us, he couldn't do that."

His take on the backlash to his comments at the march was reminiscent of Tarver's take on fans who think they're doing players a favor. "I think what is uncomfortable for many white people here is Black people that don't need them," he said. "It's not like they can tell me I'm not an LSU Tiger. You can't tell me I didn't bleed on that field for four years. You can't tell me that I don't have a degree from that school. You can't tell me that I haven't represented it well both on the field and off the field. And so there's really nothing you can do with me."

Clark was also part of a group that conducted a "racial climate" survey of LSU athletic employees. I asked him about the frequently seen talking point about sports creating understanding between people of different backgrounds. "Just because you are around another ethnicity all the time doesn't mean you learn to like a person," he said. "What you learn to do is win with them. And so I think that's a misconception about it. They don't learn to accept one another; they learn to tolerate one another."

———◆———

If Orgeron had learned anything from the Fox appearance and the march, it was not in evidence on the morning of game day, when his guest for the team's traditional "Tiger Walk" into the stadium was Republican Louisiana representative and House minority whip Steve Scalise, an ally of Trump's in his efforts to overturn the 2020 election.

That this event was taking place in the morning at all was something that most of the people I'd talked to had apologized for. The LSU-Florida game had been relegated to a rare and locally despised 11:00 a.m. kickoff because of LSU's national irrelevance during the 2021 season, and it was emphasized to me that the tailgate scene would have been exponentially more crowded, high energy, and high alcohol if the team was playing better.

I arrived to PodKatt's setup around 8:00 a.m. One of his friends, Zach, had already been there for an hour preparing the food (grits and grillades, which were little pork medallion things in sauce that had been simmered for three hours). They had set up the frame for their tent the afternoon before, as per tradition. I was surprised to hear that there was no reservation system for tailgating spots, even though a great deal of it took place right on campus, between buildings and on lawns. It was all done on the honor system and with an informal understanding of whose stuff got to go where.

I had a large morning beer and ate a doughnut. I wasn't that hungry yet because the night before I had eaten all of a takeout barbeque dinner from a restaurant called City Pork that I later realized was probably supposed to be for two people. I had surmised correctly that I would be able to get tickets for free by showing up and asking around, and I was given one in the upper deck. The stadium is an old-fashioned concrete double-decker with some nice flourishes, most notably the cutout letters that spell out WELCOME TO DEATH VALLEY in a kind of 1950s space-laser font between the first and second decks. (It looks extremely cool on TV during big night games.) The structure is located right up against campus, rising across a narrow street from some academic buildings, and the main route to it from the north ends in a glade of trees between the stadium gates and the expansive outdoor habitat where a live tiger hangs out. (The campus tiger has been a tradition since 1936. His name is Mike.)

LSU had given me a press box pass (Michigan let me into the one press conference but otherwise told me I was on my own), so I hung around there for a while and basked in the celebrity experience of sitting one folding table over from ABC play-by-play man Sean McDonough. He was looking at some papers. In upper deck section 618, the crowd was sparse enough that it felt more like being at a beach than a football game. I enjoyed the pregame hype video, which is set to Garth Brooks's fiddle-featuring cover of the country song "Callin' Baton Rouge," and I especially enjoyed that, in contrast to Michigan, there is nothing in the video that conveys there is a university in Baton Rouge, or that there are universities in any way connected to the event that is about to take place.

Oddly enough, the game went very well for the Tigers. The 6:53 mark of the first quarter was the only time I heard anyone in the section scream the word *shit* toward the field. Florida was a ranked team at the time but was on the verge of having its own meltdown, which would deposit its coach on the hot seat so fast that he got fired before the year was over. It was very windy, and Florida's quarterbacks (two of them rotated) weren't great passers to begin with, so they kept throwing interceptions. When LSU had the ball, they were running effectively behind a "jumbo" package featuring a hefty walk-on tight end whose uncle, it was mentioned in the postgame press conference, is an acquaintance of Orgeron's.

Bad football teams really can keep your hopes up in a terrible way, I knew from experience. College seasons are so short and high variance, and there is just something about getting a first down or forcing the other team to punt, even once, that produces an unparalleled brain rush. You look invincible when it happens, and you can't help thinking, *Maybe we're turning it around right here in front of my eyes.* LSU wasn't doing that, we now know, but they kept the game close, although with lots of reminders of why they had lost previous games, with good plays getting taken off the board for penalties that included, in one case, a defender straddling a Florida guy after the whistle blew in a rude, quasi-sexual way.

The back-and-forth score and the endless timeouts gave me a chance to both observe and think deeply about the varieties of human posture—how we clench our legs together and lean over during suspenseful situations to, I guess, protect our valuable intestines and genitals, but we jump and/or stretch our arms upward in moments of vicarious triumph, perhaps secure in the knowledge that our bodily internals are symbolically safe. Halfway through the fourth quarter, I went back to the press box so I could use the Wi-Fi to see Orgeron's press conference. In many stadiums, the press sits on top of the second deck, basically in blimp territory, but at LSU, the box is between the lower and upper decks, and its windows can be opened to the air. It's a very good, and loud, vantage point. There were still many tens of thousands of people in the stadium, and the lower bowl was densely filled in. When Tigers senior linebacker Damone Clark intercepted a Florida pass to seal the game, the sound was concussive, a flicker of the huge energy the place is capable of under better circumstances. "Woo," I wrote in my notebook.

Back at the tailgate, Zach was rebalancing the meat-to-liquid ratio of the postgame gumbo by pouring chunks into it from an industrial-size plastic bag. The aftergate was going to continue for a while, but I had to get back to the New Orleans airport hotel for a 7:00 a.m. flight (which I would miss because I "slept in" until 5:30 and the security line turned out to be 105 minutes long. I ended up paying $400 to get on another flight out, which my wife did not know until she read this sentence during the editing process). While walking to my car, I passed another gathering at which a woman was holding a baby in a way that suggested it was her granddaughter or grandson. *That's nice,* I thought. *Football bringing generations together. The traditions of a proud and vibrant culture.* I stopped and took in the rest of the scene. Music was playing at a volume that would normally attract the attention of the police. The woman and the baby were standing underneath a flag. On the flag was a picture of an alligator. Under the alligator, it said, "Fuck around and find out." It was time to leave Louisiana.

CHAPTER
8

MICHIGAN STATE

Others looked at their neighbors and determined to live as differently as possible.

> —*Writer William Deresiewicz, in an article published by the* Atlantic *magazine on October 18, 2021, summarizing research about Native Americans in Northern California who collectively chose to emphasize values like thrift, simplicity, and hard work in contrast to the nearby tribes of the Pacific Northwest, whom they considered ostentatious and annoying.*

ON OCTOBER 29, 2021, I interviewed Brighton, Michigan, native; Michigan State University graduate; and Michigan State sports fan Tim Alberta, a staff writer for the *Atlantic* and the author of *American Carnage: On the Front Lines of the Republican Civil War and the Rise of President Trump*, at the Haymaker Public House restaurant in Ann Arbor. Michigan and Michigan State's football teams were both undefeated and preparing to play the following day in East Lansing. Through his work as a political reporter, Alberta has semi-accidentally become one of our country's leading experts on the "culture war" and the increasingly hostile divisions between rural and urban America. I felt that made him an appropriate person to comment on the rivalry between Michigan and its nearby neighbor, which was originally launched as an agricultural school. During the interview, the location feature on my phone listed our location as a Birkenstock store, which seemed to indicate that it had developed a sense of humor regarding Ann Arbor stereotypes. Our conversation has been edited for length, clarity, and to make me sound like I was being smarter than I actually was.

Ben Mathis-Lilley: How would you describe Brighton to someone who doesn't know anything about Michigan, and how you got from there to Michigan State?

Tim Alberta: Well, so there's the Brighton of my youth, and there's the Brighton of today. When I was a kid, Brighton was your quintessentially middle-class Midwestern town. White bread, medium income of maybe $50,000 or $60,000, pretty good mix of blue-collar workers and white-collar executives who commuted south to Ann Arbor, east to Detroit, west to Lansing. Because it sat right at the intersection of the I-96 and US-23 highways, it began to grow, and grow, and grow, and grow. But when I was a kid, it was like, the only restaurants were on Main Street, or it was fast food. When Chili's came to town, my brother got a job there; it was a big deal.

And that wasn't that long ago, and suddenly it just sprung up into this kind of metropolis of big communities and trophy wives and Cadillacs everywhere. And so now it's almost like an unrecognizable place for a lot of us who grew up there. But as a kid, the first thing you've got to understand is Brighton is right down the road from Ann Arbor, so proximity-wise, that's your natural rooting interest. But as a little kid, Saturday afternoon, ABC comes on, and you see the winged helmets, and Bob Griese's on the call with Brent Musburger, and it's just like, what could be better? And so I was a big Michigan fan, my whole family was. And it never even entered into my mind as a kid that I would probably never attend the University of Michigan.

BML: Why not?

TA: I mean, it probably wasn't until high school when I really recognized the sort of relationship between a school like U of M and academic excellence and the grades that would be necessary to get in.

BML: Were you not an A student?

TA: Not at all. I was like a solid B-minus student. So a couple of things started to happen. I'll tell you the most condensed version of it possible. I've got three brothers. Two of us never went to college, and then two of us did. And I'm the youngest. My older brother went to community college, and then he transferred to Michigan State. And that was the first time I ever even entertained the idea of going to Michigan State. Because again, you grow up so close to Ann Arbor, and you see maize and blue everywhere, and I was like, "Why is he going to Michigan State?" And he's six years older than me. So when I graduated high school, I didn't have the money to go off to a four-year school right away without taking out a bunch of loans. I also didn't have great grades, and so I went to community college also.

BML: Where at?

TA: At Schoolcraft, in Livonia [a middle-class city outside Detroit]. So what happened in that year is what really reoriented me permanently. And this might sound like it's manufactured or too good to be true, [but] it's the God's honest truth, hand on a Bible here. So when I was living at home my first year after high school, going to community college, working two jobs, I was waiting tables, and I was doing janitorial work, and trying to save up as much money as I could and trying to get a 4.0 at community college so I can transfer. And I had thought about a few different options, but Michigan was the top of the list.

And two of my good friends that I grew up with, one of whom is my best friend, they went to Michigan. And so because I lived at home, and because I got nothing to do when I'm out of work, I'd go hang out there, I'd go drive to their dorm and hang out with them. They had suitemates, they had these two suitemates, and they were these rich assholes from New York.

BML: I assumed that was where this is going.

TA: If it sounds like a caricature, well, there's a reason for it. So they had these suitemates from New York, and they were complete pricks. And the first weekend I went down there to party with my two friends . . . You're eighteen, right? You're going to go out, you're trying to meet girls, and you're finding a keg party, whatever. When I went down there and first met these guys, and they found out that I went to Schoolcraft, they called me Community College the entire weekend. First of all, it's just such an unoriginal nickname; it's not clever.

BML: It's not really even a nickname.

TA: They called me Community College. They sometimes shortened it to CC. That, I thought, might just be confined to that weekend. It wasn't.

BML: Every time you went.

TA: Every time I went, these guys called me Community College. And it was the first time, as a kid who grew up just sort of

middle-class—we didn't have money, but we weren't poor. My dad
was a pastor; my mom was a homemaker. It was the first time
that I truly became self-aware, and in some way self-conscious of
class, of my own class. And it really bothered me, in ways that, as
you can tell, are still with me. It really bothered me.

And so I went for two semesters to Schoolcraft, I got a perfect
4.0 both semesters, and I talked to counselors at both MSU and U
of M, and both of them said that they were quite confident I'd be
able to get in and transfer, but I didn't even wind up applying to
Michigan. I just applied to Michigan State, said, "I think that's
where I'd be more comfortable." And you've got to understand, up
until that point, I was not a Michigan State fan. I mean, I was not
a gung-ho, Go Green guy who grew up with that. My parents are
from Jersey; they didn't have a dog in the fight.

It was just like, I looked around [at U of M] and said, "I don't
think I belong in this place. I do belong there [at MSU]." Which is
a hell of a thing for an eighteen-year-old, nineteen-year-old to
think. And so I went to Michigan State, and I kind of never
looked back. And it's interesting, because some of my buddies at
MSU, and including some guys I wound up living with, high
school friends, would bust my chops and be like, "Dude, you were
a Michigan fan in high school." And I was like, "I was, until I
realized part of what it meant to be a Michigan fan."

Now, again, that's—it's unfair to so many people, who are
normal dudes who root for the team [and] who aren't assholes. But
all generalizations have some seed of truth to them, right? And
there's no doubt that, particularly in the manifestation of the
football program and the "little brother" stuff, there's an
arrogance there and there is an elitism there that rubs a lot of
people the wrong way, and I was one of them. [Michigan running
backs coach Mike Hart, when he was a player, described the
team's 2007 comeback victory over Michigan State like this:
"Sometimes you get your little brother excited when you're
playing basketball, and you let him get the lead, and then you

come back and take it back." Spartans head coach Mark Dantonio, then in his first season, responded, "Just remember, pride comes before the fall. This game is an important game. They want to mock us all they want to mock us. I'm telling them: it's not over. So they can print that crap all they want all over their locker room. It's not over. It'll never be over here. It's just starting." He was right.]

And part of me wishes that I was bigger than that, that it didn't get to me in the way that it does, but I never looked back from that point.

BML: If this were a prestige TV show, there would be kind of a direct line from that experience to your subject matter as a professional writer, which is these kind of cultural differences and resentments. Do you think that it's a real line, or was that actually kind of also a coincidence that you ended up writing about people who feel that the big shots look down on them?

TA: I don't know. I certainly identify with people, in any walk of life, regardless of political affiliation, who feel condescended to and treated as though they are less intelligent, less qualified. I mean, look, my first day as an intern at the *Wall Street Journal* in Washington, I'd never been to DC before, not even on like a class field trip. I got this opportunity to go intern for the *Wall Street Journal.* So I moved to DC like two weeks, maybe not even two weeks, like ten days after I graduated from Michigan State. I had saved up as much as I could from working all these different jobs I had in college, and I went out there and basically lived in a closet for a while.

But my first day on the job at the *Wall Street Journal,* their economics correspondent, whom I sat next to as an intern, took me around on the first day to introduce me to people. And after talking for just a couple of minutes, he said, "Hey, where you from?" So I told him. And he took me around the office to introduce me to people. And every desk he would stop by, he would say, "Tim comes from the University of Michigan." And it was like, I had told him Michigan State. But he must have been like, "That doesn't happen."

I busted his chops about it for years. But it was clearly a subconscious thing. And hearing this, you might think, "Man, this guy is one neurotic son of a bitch." But when you deal with enough of that stuff over a period of time, it adds up and all points in one direction in your mind. You're put in these positions time after time after time, where it becomes obvious the way in which people perceive you.

Now, I would also add, though, that I've used that to my advantage. I think it can be extremely difficult for somebody who grew up wealthy and insulated from the working class to effectively and authoritatively report on the woes of the working class.

BML: Sure.

TA: When you hang around Capitol Hill, and you realize you're definitely the only reporter there who went to community college, you—people can read you as much as you're reading them. And if you're trying to build sources, and you sit down with somebody, and you start bullshitting, they can pick up pretty quickly that you're maybe a little bit different. You can use it to your advantage.

BML: Yeah, a lot of people on Capitol Hill are not Ivy League people. Successful, very powerful people, but not Ivy League backgrounds.

TA: Because it's such a melting pot. You have people from all over the country. But the reporters covering the Hill tend to be pretty homogenous.

BML: When you said that you sometimes wish you didn't have that feeling of friction about class status stuff, it reminded me that another thing you've written about a lot is people getting carried away with their feelings of resentment. [Here I referred to the contents of an article he had written about a conservative Republican state senator and Upper Peninsula dairy farmer named Ed McBroom, who'd been scorned by some of his neighbors because he concluded that there hadn't been any fraud in the state in the 2020 election.] When you think about these concepts, how do you see them playing out in the Michigan State football and Michigan State sports ecosystem? Is it sometimes too much, or is it useful for them because it's motivating and it's differentiating?

TA: I think there's probably two things. It can get out of hand, it can get obnoxious, this feeling of being marginalized or put-upon. And particularly over the past five years, during the Trump presidency, the number of conversations I've had with friends and the family members who will, just as a default mechanism, start railing against the elites . . . in those conversations I'm like, the elites are just people who know shit, and who actually read and are intellectually curious and do their homework. In other words, there's a point to which their grievances against "the elites," in quotation marks, are real, and are understandable, and I empathize with them. But it can very quickly become a self-sustaining force in which these folks will reflexively characterize any of their own misfortune, or any disagreements they have with other people, as like, "Those people think they're better than me."

Which is, I think, really dangerous. I've operated for many years now in this very weird space where I think a lot of my friends in DC—because I've always kept my politics very guarded, partially because I have very confusing and self-contradictory politics. I'm not really ideological. But a lot of my friends in DC, just culturally, I think, assumed that I was conservative, or at least right of center, or all things being relative, to the right of where they were. And then when I would come home and go out with buddies, go to a game or go to the bars or whatever, they're like, "You're a big-city DC liberal." And so I think to myself that maybe there's some substantive truth to that as far as the relativity of politics, but I also think that those perceptions are so overwhelmingly informed by, shaped by, culture. In DC, it's like, "Oh, you're a pastor's kid from the Midwest, so . . ." And back here, it's like, "Well, yeah, you're working for the mainstream media in DC, [so] you're one of them."

BML: But as you've written about, people are starting to sort themselves in such a way that those stereotypes are more and more true. [This is called geographic polarization, which refers to specific areas becoming more politically homogenous—cities becoming more Democratic while rural areas become more Republican, for example. There is some disagreement among scholars over the extent to which it's driven by conscious choices rather than being the by-product of other factors.]

TA: That's exactly right. So the football part of it is interesting, because I was thinking about this on the way over here. I don't feel any of the animosity for Michigan's basketball program that I feel for Michigan's football program. It is funny, right? But I think it's probably kind of telling at a certain level. Even though Michigan has gotten very good, even though I felt threatened by them competitively, I never disliked them. Matter of fact, I liked a lot of their players a lot, and I liked the way they played. And I even found myself sort of rooting for them when they played Louisville for the national title. Because I just didn't feel any of that animosity. But the football thing, if there's a word that is commonly and, in my view, appropriately applied to the Michigan football program, it's arrogance. There's an arrogance, there's an entitlement, there's a belief that "We are the rightful inheritors of this game, and how dare you, little brother, in-state rival, how dare you think that you can challenge us?"

There is, institutionally, in the water at University of
Michigan, a feeling of superiority to Michigan State University.
That is not debatable. And there is, institutionally, in the water at
East Lansing, a feeling of an inferiority complex relative to the
University of Michigan. That's just, it's not debatable; it's there, it's
real. And so to have any—let me frame it this way, because I
think this is probably helpful. The Michigan football team has
not won the Big Ten since 2004, right?

BML: I'm well aware, yeah.

TA: You're well aware. And yet every single season, the hype, and
the hyperbole, and the expectations, and the hometown coverage
of Michigan is just absolutely nauseating. And it's not just
nauseating; it's so wildly disproportionate to what the results
themselves would warrant. Now, on the other side of the ledger,
Michigan State University, in that same period, since 2004, has
been an objectively superior football program. I mean, there's just
no disputing that.

BML: True. [After the 2007 "little brother" back-and-forth,
Michigan State had won seven of eight games in the rivalry. Pride
had indeed cometh before the fall.]

TA: Yet Michigan State earns none of the glowing coverage; none
of the national talk shows or podcasts are discussing Michigan
State, even when they're really good, even when they're going to
the Playoff. If Michigan had gone to the Playoff, the coverage
would've felt like Bo Schembechler had been reincarnated. I
understand that branding is a big part of college athletics, and I
understand that Michigan has a national brand, arguably the
biggest national brand. I don't begrudge them that; that's not their
fault. But at a certain point, you do look around and say, "Why is
it that Jim Harbaugh, in his seventh year—who's never beat Ohio
State, who's never even gone to Indianapolis [site of the Big Ten

Championship Game] to play for a Big Ten title, much less won a Big Ten title—why does this guy get the pass that he gets?"

Now, I think in fairness, just in the past year or so, it's finally started to catch up to him a little bit. But the coverage of Michigan football, by the local guys and by the national guys, is just, it's delirious. You look around, and you're like, "Are they watching the same thing I'm watching? How is this possible?" That part of it I think specifically also gnaws at the Michigan State Spartan fanbase, because it's a little bit like those kids who were my friends' suitemates at U of M; it would basically be the equivalent of those guys going out into the real world, and sucking at their job, but Mommy and Daddy keep propping them up and paying their bills because that's what they were born into, versus me, the kid who had none of those advantages busting my ass and being successful, but nobody really cares. Is it whiny and insecure and pathetic to give voice to that? Yeah, probably, a little bit. But it's human.

BML: I have developed a bit of a theory. Or it's just a realization. I started this project thinking college football is where you go to see the values that you believe in represented, which is the idea, at least, if you go back to the 1900s or Teddy Roosevelt, the concept was that it's not just football, it's manhood, and discipline, and so forth, all those things people still talk about today. So I was thinking of the project as this thing of, people want to see their best qualities demonstrated, and that's why they put on the colors and go and cheer and chant and everything. But I think one thing that's been interesting is if you actually think about the reality of what people experience while they're watching sports, just as often, if not more often, they're angry at themselves, and they're angry at their worst tendencies. So all those things that you're saying about Michigan are things that I've already heard someone say about Michigan. It's a lens through which you see, when you're winning, your best qualities, and when you're losing, everything you said. I could go through hundreds of emails with my friends about how arrogant Michigan is.

On the flip side of this, we're talking with typical Michigan narcissism about Michigan State and how it sees itself in that kind of underdog role, but what is the positive, constructive version of how Michigan State sees itself?

TA: So it is one of the great public universities in the world. It can get lost, of course, in the haze of being a party school, and the excitement of being an elite basketball program, and a rising and exciting football program. All of that stuff, but academically, it's a Big Ten school. Michigan State is a renowned institution academically. It has one of the biggest populations of international students of any school in the United States, kids from all over the world come to study, undergraduate and especially graduate programs. It has the single biggest study abroad program of any university in the United States. They send more kids to study abroad than any school in the country. They have academic programs, particularly the packaging comes to mind as the biggest in the country. [I can confirm that you always hear about their package engineering program.] Their prelaw program is renowned. They have a very good journalism school with a lot of very successful alumni.

But I think that's what adds to the exasperation for the Michigan State fans is you feel like you're defending something that you shouldn't have to defend. Is it true that you can get into Michigan State with grades that wouldn't get you into University of Michigan? Yes. That is true. Michigan is an unbelievable school, period, full stop. Nobody's ever said that they weren't, though—that's the thing. This whole idea that like, "Oh, if you went to Michigan State, it's because you couldn't get in anywhere else." Like some kid at Michigan State misspelled a sign on ESPN one day, and it became internet fodder forever for Michigan fans.

Now, again, some of that is just good-natured rivalry shit, who cares. But again, it's like, there are all these people from Michigan State who have excelled and made wonderful contributions to the world, and who are made to feel like, almost for sport, that they went to this backwater school.

BML: Right, you wouldn't make the same jokes about the University of Iowa, or Purdue.

TA: Of course not, right? And so it's interesting. And again, I mean, as we mentioned a minute ago, you don't make the same associations basketball-wise. And I think, I do think there's something about football. Like, okay, if your team has a last-minute shot to make in basketball, you're down one, and they run a play that you don't like, and your team misses, and you're angry about it afterward. You're angry at a certain tactical level. But if your football team has fourth and one, and they go with a shotgun, and the play gets blown up by the line, you're mad not just at a tactical level but at a cultural level, and it's like an identity thing.

BML: Yep.

TA: In football, they talk all the time about, "What's the identity of your team?" You don't hear that in other sports very much. You don't hear that in baseball. And I've spent so much time in the last few years thinking, whenever I've been at Trump events, and you see everybody decked out in their garb—Trump hats, Trump scarves, Trump shirts, Trump flags—you look at that, and what they . . . "Hey, this is a lot like a sporting event." But then you go to a sporting event, and you actually think, "Hey, this is a lot like politics."

BML: Sure. [I was annoyed that he had just casually stated the thesis of this book, which I'd been trying for four years to boil down into a few sentences, off the cuff.]

TA: Because it's identity. I went to this gun show up in Birch Run a couple of years ago, a huge gun sale, the Mid-Michigan Gun and Knife Show. It's big: they had, like, twelve miles of tables inside this expo center. There was as much Trump stuff for sale there as there were firearms and munitions. And as I spent the weekend up there, talked to people, I think more people bought Trump stuff than bought guns. And you realize that, like, "Oh, this thing actually has less to do with guns than it has to do with shared identity." And I think football more than any other sport operates that way.

BML: Yeah. And Michigan–Ohio State gets the attention, and obviously has its own dimensions, but as someone who grew up in Michigan, the one where there's really rubber meeting the road, as far as people feeling like their identities are on the line, is Michigan–Michigan State. Like if Ohio State beats Michigan, which they always do, it bothers me as a sports fan, but I don't feel personally implicated by it. But every time Michigan State beats Michigan, I feel a little bit like I, personally, lost the game, you know?

TA: I do.

———◆———

The idea that Alberta and I were dancing around while drinking high-ABV beer at noon on a Friday wasn't quite that the Michigan–Michigan State rivalry is part of the "rivalry" between Democrats and Republicans in contemporary American politics. Michigan's Democratic governor, Gretchen Whitmer, is a graduate of Michigan State, while the pro-Trump chair of its state Republican Party is a University of Michigan regent named Ron Weiser, who, in March 2021, casually listed "assassination" as one of the ways that GOP representatives who voted to impeach Trump could be removed from office. ("While I should have

chosen my words more carefully, anyone who knows me under-
stands I would never advocate for violence," he subsequently said.)
It was more that the direction of American politics—its tone and
the issues that most deeply animate people to choose the side they
do—was predicted by the way Americans have clustered into college football fan groups for decades.

Basically every college football rivalry is between one school
whose fans treat their rivals like hillbillies or townies and a second
school whose fans think the first school's fans are condescending,
soft-handed rich kids. The dynamic can exist between a "farm"
school and a school for the local gentry, like Auburn–Alabama, or
a public school and an expensive private school, like UCLA–USC.
Ole Miss fans call their rivalry with Mississippi State "culture
versus agriculture." Even Harvard's student paper, in my recollec-
tion, traditionally describes its football team's many victories over
Yale as a demonstration of "the difference between the ninety-
ninth and ninety-eighth percentiles." When I was going to school
there, you could also buy shirts that depicted the Yale bulldog
mascot fellating seventeenth-century historical figure and school
namesake John Harvard, which was a bit of a mixed message.
Does it really demonstrate superior social status that a dog gave
you a blow job? I don't know, but either way, I have one of the
shirts.

Anyhoo, the aforementioned Land-Grant Act gave federal
public land to individual states in exchange for agreements to set
up universities that would specialize in "Agriculture and Mechanic
Arts." These land-grant colleges—including Auburn, Mississippi
State, and Ohio State—were often located in the vicinity of older
liberal arts schools. The snob versus slob dynamic in college football was destiny.

A more recent phenomenon, though, is the connection on a
national level between geography, college football achievement,
and political partisanship. As Alberta and I discussed, Americans'

political preferences have become more correlated with whether they live in urban or rural areas and, for white people, whether they have a college degree. This has been accelerated by Trump's polarizing nature and has made some states more red (Republican) and some more blue (Democratic) in presidential races. The ones that have gone red, most significantly, are Ohio and Florida. Those that have gotten bluer include Virginia, New Jersey, and Colorado. Universities in Ohio and Florida have won recent national football championships. Universities in those other states have not. Between 2005 and 2020, in fact, every national title was won by a team from a state that Trump won in the most recent presidential election. (The then-president actually attended the January 13, 2020, LSU–Clemson national championship game in New Orleans, where he was greeted with what one newspaper account called "overwhelming enthusiasm.")

Many of those titles were won in Alabama, which has been solid red for four decades. But at the time some of the teams in the other states won the championships—Florida in 2008, Florida State in 2013, Ohio State in 2014—their states had been Democratic in the most recent presidential race. (Louisiana, even, was a swing state as recently as the 1990s.) But when Trump came to prominence, he solidified the college football belt for Republicans—and he did it, as Alberta alluded to, by playing to the same feelings that have fueled football passion at land-grant colleges, and in the South generally, for years. His base voters are white people who don't have a college degree and feel that because of that, among other reasons, they've been marginalized and looked down on. And a funny fact is that states whose residents have fewer college degrees on a per capita basis tend to be better at college football. Among states to win an NCAA football championship in that 2005–2020 window, Florida had the highest portion of residents with at least a bachelor's degree at about 31 percent. That figure is twenty-ninth out of the fifty states.

A somewhat related development is an increase in what's called "negative partisanship." In 1980, Americans who identified themselves as either Democrats or Republicans, when asked how "favorable and warm" they felt toward the other party on a scale of zero to one hundred, gave answers that averaged out to just under fifty. That number is now below thirty. Voters are increasingly motivated by being mad at the other guy, something that is often attributed to social media because services like Facebook and Twitter make it so easy to amplify the dumbest and worst things the other guy is doing. There's not necessarily evidence that social media makes people more hostile themselves, but it does allow them to see many more hostile statements and interactions between other people than they would have otherwise, which contributes to a general feeling that everything is nasty and bad. This negativity extends beyond politics. As MSNBC host and writer Chris Hayes has put it, the internet is like a pair of supersensitive animal ears that allows us to hear every negative comment anyone else in the world makes about us (or about something we like).

Alberta had made reference to this phenomenon in a way that made me feel a little guilty when he mentioned "some kid at Michigan State" who "misspelled a sign on ESPN" and got made fun of for years. I didn't remember that incident, but I immediately thought about a picture of a car in Ann Arbor on which someone, presumably a State fan, spray-painted the word(?) STAEE after the Spartans' 2010 victory over Michigan. This item of graffiti has become a canonical image among Michigan fans of a certain age and level of onlineness, and I've laughed at it a lot over the years. I'm laughing at it right now! STAEE. In the photo, it even looks like they tried to correct the first E to a T afterward.

STAEE speaks to a problem: despite having ongoing social and professional relationships with a large handful of Michigan State graduates who are to a person smarter, more successful, and kinder than I am, my feelings about Michigan State as an institution mostly revolve around seeing Michigan people on Twitter retweet the dumbest shit their dumbest fans say and do. Or alternately, in thinking about the Michigan State program's low moments from the football rivalry, like the 2011 game in which its team committed six personal fouls, including one called against a defender who grabbed Michigan quarterback Denard Robinson's helmet and pulled it so his head and neck twisted around grotesquely—while Robinson was lying on the ground, after the play was over. After that game, Dantonio's defensive coordinator at the time, Pat Narduzzi, said dirty play had been the plan: "That's what we tried to do, sixty minutes of unnecessary roughness." (He subsequently said he had been "kind of joking" when he made the comment and did not encourage cheap shots.) During the 2017 game, a Spartan defensive back made a choking gesture at a Michigan player who'd dropped a potentially game-saving pass; before the 2018 game, State's team (with Dantonio present) did a pregame ritual called "the Spartan Walk" in such a way as to "accidentally" run into a few of Michigan's players while they were stretching.

It made me mad. I liked when Harbaugh's teams beat Dantonio twice on the road at Spartan Stadium, in 2016 and 2018, and then at the Big House in 2019 by a score of 44-10, in a season that ended up being Dantonio's last. He went out on the bottom, as far as the rivalry was concerned. Good! Negative partisanship!

On the Saturday morning of this year's game, I had gotten in touch with an MSU graduate and Kalamazoo, Michigan, ICU doctor (we'll call him "Dave") who invited me and my high-school friend Tim—not Tim Alberta—to his parents' tailgate in East Lansing. Dave's dad is such a Spartan fan that when he and his wife retired, they purchased a tasteful cottage-style home in the heart of the East Lansing student quarter. At a house across the street, there were about forty young people drinking and playing beer pong in the front yard. But at Dave's parents' place, there were lawn chairs and a tent set up over a big spread of food on a lawn surrounded by nicely tended hedges. "So they go somewhere south during the winter?" Tim asked Dave about his parents.

"No, they come here and go to basketball games," Dave said. Dave's father's sister and her husband were also there. They owned another one of the houses across the street.

Dave's uncle was a supply-chain manager for a manufacturing company. His dad was retired from Chrysler. I thought about what Alberta had said. According to the most recent statistics I could find, 54 percent of living degreed alumni of Michigan State live in Michigan, as compared with around 33 percent for U of M. Many Michigan graduates take jobs elsewhere in high finance, computer science, media, and so forth—things that put the university on the map nationally. MSU excelled in areas like engineering, teaching, and business administration—disciplines that were often applied locally. They made the state work.

But, whatever. I still wanted to win the game.

———— ◆ ————

Tim and I were given beers for our coat pockets and walked toward the campus and the stadium. The air was chilly and wet, more misting than raining; the whole day felt like the moment your skin makes contact with the peripheral spray of a shower in a cold house. The game was scheduled for noon, and it was the first one I'd been to during the season that could be described as having an electric atmosphere. Both ESPN's *College GameDay* and Fox's *Big Noon Kickoff* national pregame shows were broadcasting on location. Tickets were stupidly expensive. I paid $450 each for a pair in the lower endzone. Disgusting.

MSU's tailgate scene is LSU-style, with many pockets of activity in various parking lots and quads and apartment complexes. We found something called the "Meijer Fan Experience" near the stadium, which was a banner that read MEIJER FAN EXPERIENCE above what, as far as I could tell, was just a big field of mud. (Meijer is a local superstore chain. West Michigan Republican representative Peter Meijer, a family heir, voted to impeach Donald Trump, which means that he is one of the people whom Ron Weiser was referring to in his "assassination" remarks, which as Weiser has clarified, are not to be understood as advocating violence.) The *GameDay* set was on a nearby area covered in artificial turf; it was bigger than I expected, with an elevated stage and multistory lighting trusses. In context, it looked like a castle surrounded by peasants celebrating the harvest. In every direction, there were people coming and going and an astounding number of empty beer cans, cups, and other items of trash on the ground. As you walked, you passed between zones of body-vibrating bass. This sensory assault combined with the brain haze induced by the beers in a way I found pleasingly disorienting. I peed behind a shipping container that, for some reason, was part of the Meijer Fan Experience.

Game time approached. Tim and I walked to our gate by passing along the side of the stadium underneath the bleachers. Spartan Stadium has a renovated structure of offices and boxes on one side that looks like an Embassy Suites, but otherwise it's just two concrete slabs that extend up and up above the mostly nondescript, low-lying, flat, gray municipality of East Lansing. I mean this as a compliment. The effect is to make you think, *These men and women are a harder people than we are.* No one wants to fight a Serbian.

Inside the stadium, everyone was packed together fifteen minutes before kickoff. In more vertical stadiums like Michigan State's, it feels like the crowd is on top of the players, and the green of the field and the yellow, white, and green of the uniforms stood out luminescently from the Michigan mudscape. The local pregame hype tradition is that a PA announcer reads a description of the weather, which is usually bad and was, as mentioned, bad on this day as well, which he ends by concluding, along with the rest of the crowd, that "It's a Beautiful Day for Football!"

I expected Michigan to win. Michigan State was, in fact, undefeated, but in a flimsy sort of way, with multiple close wins against not-so-great teams like Indiana. Michigan had the better numbers. There had been more rumblings, led by Webb of 247Sports, that the tantalizing freshman quarterback, McCarthy, could get an even bigger role on the offense. Was he going to be a superstar by the end of the year? Maybe Michigan would win in a blowout. What if it was a blowout? That would be great!

On Michigan's first possession, Cade McNamara threw a pass to a previously little-used true freshman wide receiver named Andrel Anthony on a crossing route from Michigan's own seven-yard line. From our seats behind the play, it looked like McNamara was throwing into a maze. There were four Michigan receivers guarded by seven defenders. But it was a perfect pass between two Spartans, past another, and right over a ducking referee. Anthony ran past the MSU defensive backs, who seemed as surprised as everyone else to see him in the game, for a ninety-three-yard touchdown.

Michigan would hit a number of big passes like this in the middle of the field, and the team moved the ball more consistently than Michigan State overall, but the Spartans made more tough, gritty plays. ("Grit" is football parlance for "playing well without looking good." "Tough" means "gritty.") Over the course of the game, Michigan settled for field goals after failing to convert a third and seven, a third and three, a third and six, and a third and eight. Michigan State, by contrast, gained first downs or scored on a fourth and one, a fourth and four, a third and three, and another third and three. Michigan violated one of the canonical rules of playing a highly motivated underdog in a volatile environment: you can't let them hang around. "You can't let them hang around like this," Tim and I said to each other.

Sitting to my right was a fiftysomething Michigan State alumnus who said he was a middle-school physical education teacher in a small town near the Indiana border. He was dismayed at how long his team's quarterback, Payton Thorne, was holding on to the ball. On one play on our end of the stadium, Thorne dropped back, surveyed the field, rolled out to his left, kept looking around for a while, and, if I recall correctly, ran out of bounds. "Throw the fucking ball!" my neighbor screamed.

His wife turned toward him as if to disapprove of his obscene exclamation, or so I thought. "He needs to throw the ball," she said.

Just before the half, David Ojabo, coming from the offense's left, sacked Thorne near Michigan State's own end zone while hacking the ball out of his hand with a violent chop. Aidan Hutchinson, coming from the right, jumped on it for what would have been a touchdown that put Michigan up 27-14. But after an extremely long video replay, the referees working the game decided that Thorne had held on to the ball long enough for his shin to have touched the very tippy tops of the grass blades on the field before it came loose. The play was ruled a sack, not a fumble, and the touchdown was taken off the board. It was a devastating decision.

In the second half, Michigan took a 30-14 lead but developed an increasingly concerning problem on defense. That problem was Michigan State running back Kenneth Walker III. Michigan State's new coach, Mel Tucker, had come up with a good solution to the aforementioned depletion of his roster and of the local-talent problem that Midwestern teams face in general. For years, NCAA athletes were penalized if they transferred from one school to another by being required to sit out a year of competition. The NCAA finally changed this rule in 2021, enabling more players to move more freely. Most programs took in a few transfer players at spots where their roster depth wasn't great. Tucker and Michigan

State took twenty, including Walker, who had previously played for Wake Forest.

It turned out to be the right choice for him, as he had the best season of any running back in the country. Michigan's defensive linemen were good, but watching them try to tackle Walker was like watching henchmen trying to corner Spider-Man. U of M would get a defender in the space where the play was headed, but then Walker would zip laterally ten feet with a sideways leap and suddenly be running full speed into the secondary on the other side of the field.

MSU compounded Michigan's trouble by sprinting up to the new line of scrimmage after big Walker plays to run another play immediately, often an "outside zone" run, which, to keep it relatively simple, is where the running back and the offensive line sort of casually migrate toward the sideline together before the running back decides where to go. It forces the opposing team to follow the offense and figure out what spaces they have to defend on the fly. Michigan had a lot of trouble with this, particularly because they kept trying to substitute new linemen onto the field in between plays. So a group of giant guys would run on and get set for less than a second before they had to all start running again, and then Walker would zoom by them. There would have been a slapstick Road Runner effect to it had I been in the mood for mirth and revelry.

Walker had five touchdowns in the game, which is too many. Five touchdowns! Come on! I tried to react to each of his absurd runs, as the score got closer and closer, by shrugging my shoulders and sighing magnanimously, as if to say, Well, what are you gonna do? But in my heart, things were bad. "This is not going to be good for the narrative," Tim said. It was true. Fox was almost certainly updating the Graphic of Despair. With seven minutes left and Michigan leading by only three, J. J. McCarthy went into the game for McNamara, who was being checked by members of the medical staff. He attempted to hand off to Blake Corum at around midfield, but neither player held on and the ball dropped straight down onto the ground. Michigan State recovered and then took a 37-33 lead. That would end up being the final score. Tim got an alert on his phone for an email from one of our friends on the chain. "Sam Webb can kiss my ass," it said.

It had been mentally and physically exhausting watching the game. By the beginning of the fourth quarter, I felt like taking a nap. We'd been up since 6:30 a.m., thinking about nothing but football, and it was already starting to get dark. I could not imagine what it felt like to have been playing or coaching under the circumstances, to the extent that instead of being angry, I was impressed by how long Michigan had stuck around and how close they had come to winning. "Hostile environment" doesn't do justice to the fury of a home team comeback in front of seventy-five thousand people. Before every crucial Michigan down, the PA would play an audio clip that sounded like this: "BWAHHH-AHH-UHHH / BWA-BWA-BWA BWA-BWA-BWA BWA-BWA-BWA BWAHHHHH / BWA-BWA-BWA BWA-BWA-BWA BWA-BWA-BWA BWAHHHHH." I haven't been able to determine when or how this set of noises was composed. I assume it's from a movie or song that is popular with teens. But it sounds like a dinosaur coming to get you and is very scary. When Michigan State made a big play, because of the slight delay created by sound traveling from the other sections, the roar wouldn't hit all at once but rather came as an escalating shockwave that built and whipped around from the other side of the stadium. (You don't notice this effect as much at a home game, I think, because you're also yelling.) Being a visiting fan felt like being on a really small ship that had really angered the ocean god.

During one Michigan third down in the fourth quarter, I took a 360-degree video to document the frenzy. At the bottom of the screen was Jim Harbaugh, a speck in the maelstrom. He was going to be back on the ol' hot seat. In that moment, from that distance, the idea of blaming one person for the outcome of a football game—which involves thousands of interactions between dozens of players during a three-and-a-half-hour marathon of shifting momentum and randomness—seemed absurd. What is one man against the storm? But when the gods get angry, the people have to make a sacrifice.

CHAPTER

9

FLORIDA ATLANTIC VS. MARSHALL

Ben Mathis-Lilley: As a fan, just as a person, how does that play into your fandom and your love of the sport? How does it complicate that? How do you, I guess, compartmentalize the ugly side of it with the part of it you love?

Richard Johnson: I mean, I'm Black in America. If I didn't compartmentalize racism, I wouldn't be able to live here.

THE OWL TIME STORE, a leading distributor of Florida Atlantic University Owls spiritwear and memorabilia, is part of the same retail space as a running shoe vendor and a shop that restrings tennis rackets. The three entities share about fifty feet of storefront in a strip mall between a State Farm office and Boca Surf and Sail on the four-lane Federal Highway in Boca Raton, the famed retirement destination about an hour north of Miami.

I'd arrived in South Florida for a trip of about thirty-six hours to see Willie Taggart, who'd become the head coach at Florida Atlantic after a tenure in charge of Florida State that was very eventful and very short. Owl Time was the first place I'd gone after leaving my hotel room, which can only be described as "a bit damp," and I was already realizing that I was overdressed by virtue of having pants on. It was not the kind of big-time environment most of the people who had followed Taggart's career expected him to be part of at this stage in his life.

According to accounts in the press, Taggart's long journey to Owl territory actually started with a phone call from Jim Harbaugh. Taggart was a high school quarterback in Bradenton, Florida, which is in the Tampa area, in the early '90s. Jim Harbaugh was still playing for the Chicago Bears but was working as a volunteer assistant for his father Jack's Western Kentucky team during his downtime. Jim was assigned to recruit Taggart, which he successfully did. Taggart became a star for WKU and immediately joined its coaching staff after graduating. When Jim Harbaugh was hired at Stanford, Taggart joined him as an assistant, went from there back to Western Kentucky for the head job, and from that gig was hired to coach the University of South Florida, a Division I program (technically, they call Division I the "Football Bowl Subdivision" now) that, confusingly, is in Tampa. (It's not even a degree of latitude closer to the equator than the University of Central Florida, which is in Orlando. When USF was founded in 1956, the combined population of what is now thought of as South Florida—mainly Dade, Broward, and Palm Beach Counties along the Atlantic Ocean—was only around seven hundred thousand. It's currently more than six million.)

In his fourth year at USF, Taggart's team went 10-2, and he was hired by Oregon, a major-conference school only three seasons removed from having played in the national championship game. Not long before that hire was announced, Taggart told college football writer Steven Godfrey that his goal in football was to become "the first African American head coach to win a national title." Oregon was somewhere that could happen. Its roster included a sophomore quarterback named Justin Herbert, who's now a star in the NFL and whose assets—quick feet, crazy arm strength, being very tall—made him an ideal fit for the offense Taggart had developed as a coach, which will give a quarterback as much workload both as a runner and as a deep passer as he can handle. But after one okayish season in 2017, during which Herbert missed a month with an injury, Taggart left Oregon for Florida State.

It was an eyebrow-raising move. He had four years left on his Oregon contract, and Florida State's program had been regressing on the field and making national news for a pattern of player arrests and incidents that probably should have led to arrests but were allegedly ignored or covered up. Taggart justified the decision by calling the position his "dream job." At his introductory press conference, he choked up as he talked about growing up in a family of Florida State fans. "You would've thought everyone in that house graduated from FSU, and none of us did," he said. "I'm in! I'm in now!"

Twenty-three months later, he was fired. The team went 5-7 in 2018, Taggart's first year, and hadn't seemed to improve over the course of the season, losing its final game by twenty-seven points. The next year, after a seventeen-point loss to the University of Miami in early November dropped its record to 4-5, Taggart was terminated. FSU's athletic director told the press he had concluded Taggart would not be successful as coach and that as such, there was no reason not to start looking for a replacement immediately despite his still being owed more than $15 million. "We didn't really see any upside to waiting," the AD said.

Taggart had been Florida State's first Black head football coach, and it's rare for college coaches, even the ones who start poorly, to be terminated before they've worked three full seasons, much less two. FSU is in Tallahassee, in the northern part of Florida, which is generally whiter and more conservative than its other regions. Its most important football figure, longtime coach Bobby Bowden, endorsed and appeared with Donald Trump during the 2016 campaign, in which Trump's support from white supremacists and history of suggesting Barack Obama was an African-born Muslim received a great deal of attention. After a loss in November 2018, a Florida State fan posted an image on Facebook of Taggart's face photoshopped onto a picture of a real-life lynching. (The individual was then reportedly fired from his job at the Hilton hospitality corporation.) Taggart's record at the program was 9-12, while his white successor, Mike Norvell, is 8-13 and still employed.

So there was circumstantial evidence that Taggart had gotten a raw deal because he was Black. When I asked reporters who knew the state—like Gainesville native and *Sports Illustrated* staff writer Richard Johnson, who is quoted earlier, and Bud Elliott—they noted that he had also made mistakes on his own. He did not recruit that well, may have publicly set expectations too high given the state of disorganization in which his predecessor (Jimbo Fisher) had left the roster, and reportedly did not run the tightest of ships as far as things like making sure practice time was used efficiently. (That said, Johnson was not suggesting that race did not play a role: "Would a white coach have been fired at the point he was fired? My answer will always be no.")

It was also emphasized to me that Florida State is not an institution that is prepared to accept a sustained downturn in football success, even when compared to somewhere like LSU. Between 1905 and 1947, FSU was exclusively a women's school—at one point, it had the maximally generic name of "Florida Female

College." Its alumni and donor networks are relatively small, and its football history is short. (Said Johnson, "Historically, the governors and the congressmen and the state reps and stuff go to Florida. They don't go to Florida State.") A great deal of its sports funding comes from a good ol' boy organization of boosters that until recently operated as a distinct legal entity outside the control of the athletic department. Jimbo Fisher left for Texas A&M in 2017, despite having won a national title at Florida State in 2013, after an extensive and petty series of feuds—documented in a 2020 ESPN article—with administrators and boosters over what he felt was inadequate support.

FSU still does not have one of the vaunted "standalone" football facilities that Saban asked for (and received) at LSU in the early aughts. It didn't have a practice field with a roof over it until 2013, and as Johnson pointed out, it rains in Florida at about 3:30 p.m. every day during the summer, which made for a practical hindrance more significant than most programs at its level of aspiration are used to dealing with. (LSU's indoor field was completed in 1991.) In 2019, FSU sold just over thirty thousand season tickets—fifty-four thousand fewer than Michigan sold after one of its worst seasons ever. In this environment, there may not have been any coach who could have survived the bottoming out that was inevitable at the time when Taggart took the job. Mike Norvell, as mentioned, is not doing too well either.

The irony is that the state of Florida does, or did, have a history of institutional college football success and continuity that dates back to the first half of the twentieth century. But it's not a history that involves many white players, because its colleges were segregated. The public university to which Black students were restricted was Florida A&M, or FAMU, which is also located in Tallahassee. The FAMU Rattlers were vastly better on the field than their white counterparts at the University of Florida, claiming three Black college national titles before the first year (1952) that the Gators finished a season ranked in the AP poll. Once it went co-ed, Florida State launched its own team but only recorded ten winning seasons in major-college ball before Bowden was hired, by which time FAMU had claimed another seven championships.

The Rattlers, more than their all-white state-school peers, created what University of Kentucky history professor Derrick White refers to as a "sporting congregation" in his 2019 book *Blood, Sweat, and Tears*, a history of that football program and its longtime coach Jake Gaither. FAMU alums became coaches at Black high schools and funneled their athletes back to the university at the same time that its legend grew within a national network of Black fans and journalists. (Gaither's most well-known player was probably Bob Hayes, a Hall of Fame receiver for the Cowboys, but a number of others played in the NFL.)

By rights, from a football perspective at the very least, desegregation in the state of Florida probably should have been accomplished by allowing the best white players to have a shot at playing for Jake Gaither. Keen students of American history may surmise that this is not how things were done.

Southern white schools began recruiting Black players because the federal government was forcing them to, and to gain a competitive advantage. This motive is often said to be symbolized by USC's high-profile 42-21 victory, led by Black running back Sam "Bam" Cunningham, over all-white Alabama in Birmingham in 1970. The influence of that game is sometimes overstated, as plans for desegregation were already underway in Alabama's program and elsewhere, but it was nonetheless a much-discussed object lesson in whites-only athletic futility.

As White documented in a 2010 *Florida Historical Quarterly* article, the same head coach who had replaced the decals on the University of Florida's helmets with Confederate battle flags before the 1962 Gator Bowl against Penn State—a northern team known for having Black players—began desegregating the

Florida team in 1968. This kind of competitive escalation, in Florida and elsewhere, came at the expense of historically Black programs that already had limited resources. "Florida State was able to use this strong push to desegregate their football team as a mechanism to ramp up their competition with Florida," White told me. "Doak Campbell"—where FSU plays—"is a publicly funded stadium. The state raised money for it. And in order to do so, they underfunded Florida A&M."

White continued:

One of the chief complaints of Black coaches at the time is, "Look, we don't have any recruiting money for that." When you're talking about the very first handful of Black players, there are a number of stories—here at the University of Kentucky, during the attempts to recruit the first Black basketball player, the governor of the state was trying to woo a kid to come to University of Kentucky. That's not happening at Florida A&M. White coaches would say, "You have a better chance of being in the pros if you come to Florida," which was probably not true in the early '70s, but by 1980 probably was. "You're going to be on TV"—that part was true. Money was starting to be poured into [white] athletic departments. That's where you start to see the opening shots in that arms race of college athletics.

Desegregation scattered the sporting congregation. Bowden, whatever motivations we may understand to have been in his heart, recruited with great effectiveness across racial lines. "Bowden really thrived in going into rural Black homes," White says. "If you look at their rosters, they did really well in what would be defined as the rural parts of the state, and southern Georgia." Charlie Ward, the Heisman Trophy–winning quarterback of the first Florida State team to win the national title, is from

Thomasville, Georgia, a town of about eighteen thousand that's thirty-five miles north of Tallahassee. These players, as well as those at the private University of Miami in South Florida and (later on) at the University of Florida under Steve Spurrier, were extraordinarily successful. In the 1980s and 1990s, the three teams won a combined seven national championships. Each team had a streak of winning at least ten games per season that lasted eight seasons or longer.

Gaither had cultivated teams known for their speed, as exemplified by Hayes, who in addition to his football career won gold medals in the 100-meter dash and 4×100 relay at the 1964 Tokyo Olympics. Says White, "If you read the newspapers, every year, Gaither talked about having an 'abundance' of speed, and when he didn't feel like he had an abundance, that was the thing that made him nervous." Fast football players were a point of area pride, and that carried over, for example, to the Seminole teams that Willie Taggart rooted for in the 1980s. Bowden's most sensational player was North Fort Myers High School's Deion Sanders, who would go on to be the only player in NFL history who ranks in the all-time top ten for both touchdowns scored on punt returns and touchdowns scored on interception returns. (It helps to be fast to do these things.)

Under both Bowden and his successor, Fisher, however, whistleblower accounts and journalistic exposés also gave FSU a reputation for maintaining players' academic eligibility through fraudulent means. The school admitted to one set of violations involving twenty-three players in 2007 and was the subject of a long *New York Times* piece about allegedly plagiarized and tutor-completed work in 2017. By the year Fisher left, its academic progress rate (an NCAA measure that's slightly different than GSR) was the worst of any major-conference team. One might argue that football players should not be required to complete collegiate academic work in order to engage in what for many of them is pre-professional athletic training. But attesting to believe they should, then funneling them through bogus classes such that they leave school either with a degree that has little value or without a degree at all, is also a problematic approach.

There's a sociological concept called predatory inclusion that White raised with me. It refers to a historically dominant group incorporating representatives of a minority cohort and enjoying the benefits therefrom—in the case of college football, some of those benefits include good public relations, the prestige of winning games, and alignment with federal law—in a way that does not necessarily build the cultural or actual capital of the minority individuals involved. In his work, White draws a related distinction between desegregation, or allowing Black students to enroll in a given school, and integration, a term he argues should be applied only to situations in which those students, while expressing their "authentic selves," can become full members of collegiate life both formally and socially.

The distinction reminded me of the story of Michigan football player Willis Ward. Ward was a standout athlete from Detroit who was recruited to Michigan to run track in the early 1930s, when Michigan was ostensibly an "integrated" school but only had about a dozen Black students. Ward also joined the football team, becoming its only non-white player. In 1934, he was involved in a conflict that became part of program legend when Georgia Tech was scheduled to play in Ann Arbor but sent word that it wouldn't take the field if Ward was playing. It became a hot campus issue; some students argued that it would be better to cancel the game than to honor Georgia Tech's request, but Michigan coaches and administrators wanted to bench Ward and play. One of the leaders of the Michigan team that year was Gerald Ford. It became lore, repeated in a 2011 documentary and even alluded to in a eulogy George W. Bush gave in 2007 at Ford's funeral, that he threatened to quit the team to protest the coaches' decision only to be talked out of it by Ward, who volunteered to sit the game out in order to resolve the situation. The team, which was not a good one that year, was purportedly then so motivated to make a statement about Georgia Tech's bigotry that it dominated the Yellow Jackets for its only win of the season.

This story seems to have been quite embellished. There's no contemporary or primary evidence that Ford ever tried to quit the team. In his autobiography, he wrote merely that he was disturbed by the situation and that Ward talked him into playing, but even that version of events is suspect. In 2014, a Michigan investigative site called Washtenaw Watchdogs located 1976 and 1983 interviews with Ward, who had gone on to become a federal judge, in which he said that though he and Ford were friendly and he'd heard Ford was upset that Ward was being forced out of the Georgia Tech game, they never spoke about the situation. Ward agreed not to play, he said, because representatives of the Ford Motor Company (no relation to Gerald) promised to give him a job if he did so without complaining. Ward in fact said that the incident effectively ended his career as an athlete because he decided that it wouldn't be worth it to train for the 1936 Olympics—which were held in Nazi Germany—given the chance that he would be prevented from competing in a similar concession to racism.

Ultimately, star sprinter Jesse Owens—who, as an athlete at Ohio State, had been one of Ward's peers—did compete at the games, winning four gold medals. This is an extremely unflattering contrast for Michigan, if you think about it: Hitler couldn't stop Jesse Owens from competing, but Michigan stopped Willis Ward.

———— ◆ ————

In the South, despite concerns about the effects of concussions, data from the National Federation of State High School Associations shows football participation in most states remaining steady or increasing. The supply of football players in Florida has created entire respectable college programs where before there were not even colleges. The University of Central Florida opened to students in 1968, joined Division I-A football in 1996, and has won two big-deal New Year's Day bowl games. Florida Atlantic, where Taggart signed on a month after being dismissed at Florida State, opened in 1964 and began football life just this century when the legendary, mustachioed Howard Schnellenberger, who had coached the Baltimore Colts and University of Miami Hurricanes, gave up a second career as a bond salesman to launch its program, which joined the I-A level in 2004. (Both UCF and FAU are public universities.) In 2007, while they were still playing in temporary off-campus stadiums, the Owls beat the University of Minnesota, which has been playing football since 1882.

FAU's motive for getting into the sport, associate athletic director for communications Katrina McCormick says, is straight-forward: it wanted to be more like a regular college than a commuter school, and regular colleges have football. "The average age of the students in the early nineties was twenty-six or twenty-seven. And to create that college atmosphere, that college experience, Dr. Catanese wanted football on campus," she said. (Anthony Catanese was the school's president at the time. In 2003, a university official pleaded guilty to a misdemeanor charge of falsifying records related to $42,000 that was transferred from the school's fundraising foundation to Catanese for the purpose of buying a Corvette. The money was paid to his wife through an interior design firm, allegedly for "consulting services" related to the decoration of the president's mansion. Neither Catanese nor his wife were charged with a crime in the case. He said he believed the arrangement was legal.) "It was all done in an effort to make FAU a more traditional-type campus for freshmen, sophomores, juniors, and bring the average age of the students down. We do have a large commuter population that goes to school here, but they've also built a bunch of dorms."

McCormick says the team initially dressed for practices at Palm Beach State Junior College, because FAU didn't even have a locker room. Its record went up and down, and there was an interesting episode in 2013 when Carl Pelini—the brother of recurring college football character Bo Pelini—resigned from his job as head coach after an assistant claimed to have seen him smoking marijuana in Key West and using cocaine at an unspecified location. One week later, Pelini tried to unresign, so the school fired him instead. (He denies having used illegal drugs, and the school did not make a judgment on the merits of the assistant's claim in terminating him. Pelini later sued the assistant for defamation, but I could not find information on the outcome of the suit in the public record.) Before the 2017 season, FAU hired Lane Kiffin, a mop-headed blond shit-talker who, before he had turned thirty-nine years old, had left head coaching jobs with the Oakland Raiders and University of Tennessee under acrimonious circumstances (the acrimony mostly directed toward Kiffin by other people) and gotten personally fired by USC's athletic director after getting off an airplane in Los Angeles at 3:00 a.m.

I asked McCormick how Kiffin's hiring came together. "He really, I don't think, was interested in it at first. The president put together a team of individuals that flew up and met him. And he built a good relationship with the president and several of the members of the board of trustees and, I think, felt like they would let him run the program," she said. "He also had the ability to have a little bit of anonymity in this community because nobody was going to stop him while he was eating a burger, where any other school's fans in the SEC would. So it gave him a chance to build a winning record as a head coach, and it gave him that ability to build a staff, to show he could do it, and then to eventually take over an SEC program." In a world in which almost no one will ever admit to doing anything for any reason except "the well-being of the student-athletes," it was nice to hear someone admit to a relationship of mutual interest, though I have no reason to think that McCormick was against student well-being.

Kiffin was a big success. His FAU teams won eleven games in two of his three seasons, after which he was hired by Ole Miss, where he's also done well. Taggart, attempting a similar rehabilitation, was his replacement. (Kentucky's White, who was previously a professor at FAU, noted that hiring figures like Kiffin and Taggart, who had preexisting national reputations, is another way that FAU uses football to leverage its brand name into the broader consciousness.)

I wondered what FAU football's *thing* was, in the way that Michigan's was the combination of athletic and academic excellence, and LSU's was being the life of the party. "What the current athletic director has pushed," McCormick said, "which has really stuck longer than any other thing that we've done, is *paradise*." Slogans I saw during my time in Boca included "Winning in Paradise," "Defend Paradise," and "Mayhem in Paradise," and there's a large sign on the outside of the FAU stadium noting that the beach is 1.8 miles away.

I left Owl Time to investigate paradise, walking past condo buildings and mini-malls to Spanish River Park, a tranquil (and fairly large, given the surroundings) natural preserve between the beach and an inlet whose other bank was lined with pastel-colored luxury homes. I spent some time walking a trail through "gumbo limbo" trees, which have a haunted-forest appearance, and passed underneath a number of spiderwebs as wide as a two-lane road. At the center of each was a spider bigger than my hand. Waves from the inlet splashed up and around the trunks of the trees at the water's edge.

Then I found a sports bar called the Whistle Stop Public House, which was selling craft beer and upscale appetizers to a crowd heavy on weathered-looking guys with long hair, tattoos, and earrings. It was located between a hardware store and a pawn shop and is, I think, proof that Brooklyn food trends have spread literally everywhere. Ohio State was struggling with Nebraska on one of the TVs, which was great. I continued watching the game on my phone while I walked to FAU proper along a long access road that was clearly not designed to be walked along.

The university's website describes its campus as having "everything you would expect from a modern university," including a "movie theater complex." Its buildings reminded me of renovated airport terminals, with airy lobbies and walls of windows several stories tall. I was raised among the imposing campuses of the Midwest and Northeast and was intrigued by the idea of a university that's not supposed to make you feel anxious and intimidated. The most active FAU donor, based on building names, seems to have been Dorothy Schmidt, whose husband founded the Tractor Supply Co. home-and-garden chain before settling in Boca.

I almost stepped on an enormous lizard while staring at my phone and watching Nebraska botch its chance at an upset. The lizard and I were the only ones lingering on the quad, but students were walking by here and there toward the stadium to the north. I walked up to the parking lot, which was active, if not close to full. The closest tailgating spot to the stadium was held by a professor of criminology with ponytail-length white hair. He and his wife said they have been to every home game the school has played. "We've had some lean years," he said. I later looked up his CV, which notes (among many normal academic things) that he has been the faculty adviser for FAU's tae kwon do club for nineteen years and that he won the fall 2017 Tailgater of the Year Award.

I was pointed in the direction of the student tailgate, which was in another parking lot next to an open field on the other side of the stadium. I arrived just in time to see a guy who was probably about 250 pounds do a flying elbow drop off a cooler and through a folding table. Why was the student tailgate in this random parking lot with nothing else around it, I wondered. Why was anything down here anywhere? At the stadium, I went in through the VIP entrance, which has its own valet parking circle. There was a fully stocked bar on the fifty-yard line, where anyone who wants to can stand and watch the game from a patio just above field level. Paradise? Sure.

FAU was playing Marshall, which is in West Virginia. Both were still in competition for first place in Conference USA, a contrived interregional conference that consists of a shifting group of schools that bear no meaningful relationship to each other. FAU's stadium fits about thirty thousand people and is nice to look at, done in gleaming silver, red, and different shades of ocean blue. It was maybe one-quarter full. The members of the nursing faculty in the seats next to mine said that this was probably because it was "cold." The temperature was seventy-one degrees.

Florida Atlantic's defense and its offensive line were not great, but it had a six-foot, four-inch quarterback named N'Kosi Perry who had transferred from Miami and was immediately identifiable as a superior athlete, as well as a five-foot, five-inch running back named Johnny Ford who was extremely quick and transcendently reckless with his body in the way that great players must be. Seen in person, the best running backs look, on every play, like they would trade everything they have for another inch.

Ford kept coming out of the game, though, and threw up on the sideline. Taggart said after the game that he had the flu, which had been going around other teams in the state as well. FAU fell behind by two touchdowns. When I went back to the bar, a guy of about thirty who was wearing an expensive-looking quarter-zip fleece and a white Yankees hat was in front of me in line. In front of him was a woman who looked to be in her fifties wearing a white top and a colorful belt and wobbling a little. "She's a teacher," he said to me, having apparently just been made aware of that fact and some others. "Imagine if she was *your* teacher," he added. "You'd be illiterate."

She got to the bartender. "He's paying for my drink," she said, pointing back at the man.

"No I'm not," he said.

The Owls had chances to get in the game—three times Perry hit open receivers with long, tenderly placed deep passes only for them to drop the ball. As the 28-13 Marshall win wound down, I spent some time in the press box listening to the soothing patter of the spotters who watch each play with binoculars and a roster in order to keep statistics. After the final whistle, the opposing teams of assistant coaches, who have their own skyboxes so as to be able to see the entire field at once, met at the elevator bank and shook hands before taking separate cars down to the field. The interior of the elevator I used was completely covered from floor to ceiling in an advertisement for personal injury attorneys in Fort Lauderdale. Taggart's press conference lasted eight minutes; there were twelve people there, including me and him. He seemed anguished by the dropped passes, and tired.

CHAPTER
10

PENN STATE

Enough is enough and it might be time to stop caring about
Michigan football.

> —247Sports.com message board user Hott Karl, October 30,
> 2021, 3:57 p.m.

SOME OF THE CHOICEST MESSAGE board comments and new-thread
subject lines posted after the University of Michigan's loss to Michigan State included "Shame on this coaching staff," "Game in hand
and just choked all over themselves," "Can we get the name of the
replay official who overturned the call," and my favorite, "Back from
a weeklong ban for using a bad word about Sparty." One 247Sports
subscriber wrote that while "we always attribute obvious calls that
go against us as incompetent refferees [*sic*]," he was now wondering

if there were "something more sinister at play." Then there was Hott Karl, quoted above, who was prepared to throw it all away.

We have all been there, like Hott Karl, the Hamlet of our time, wondering whether the anguish was worth the intermittent reward. I was there myself at about 3:00 p.m. on November 13, 2021, when Penn State recovered a fumble at Michigan's sixteen-yard line with the score tied and less than seven minutes left in the game.

After a perfunctory and extremely slow-paced victory over Indiana, Michigan was playing the Nittany Lions at Beaver Stadium on that Saturday for the right to argue that its season was a modest success. A loss to Ohio State in the final game over Thanksgiving was assumed, but if Michigan could manage a victory over PSU and dispatch a weak Maryland team the week after, it would go into that game 10-1. A final regular-season record of 10-2 would very possibly mean ending the season with a top-ten ranking. That would be pretty good after the previous year's events, warranting modest optimism and conversations about "heading in the right direction." A loss to Penn State would mean 9-3, a fringe top-twenty-five ranking, and a reentry into the *Groundhog Day*–like loop of arguments about permanent mediocrity. Being ranked in the top twenty-five and winning most of your games is a weird definition of mediocrity, but it is the one Michigan fans have. I don't make the rules.

Penn State, ranked twenty-fifth going into the game, was okay. It was like Michigan teams of previous years, still a relevant enough name because of its past success and ardent following to attract some top players but not loaded or efficient enough to compete with the best programs. The university itself is a rural analogue to Michigan, a large school with a national reputation, but located in a small town that is over one hundred miles from the nearest major city. The maps claim that there is an interstate that serves State College, Pennsylvania, but I'm not buying that; I've lived my whole life in and around this part of the country, and I've never heard anyone talking about a so-called I-99. The correct way to get to Penn State is by driving for a long time down two-lane roads that pass through hills, farms, and eleven-resident roadside towns called Flapsburg Gap until, bam, right there on the next hill, there's a big football stadium—the second-largest in the United States after Michigan's, in fact.

Pennsylvania has a sneakily strong football tradition. It's the only state outside the South in which more than one college has won a national championship since integration—the University of Pittsburgh in 1976 and Penn State in '82 and '86 (with the Nittany Lions having a case for deserving a share of Nebraska's in '94 as well). It specializes in figures who have a legendary aura to them, like Tony Dorsett, Mike Ditka, Johnny Unitas, and Joe Montana.

Michigan certainly seemed intimidated by the environment and the aura on its first two possessions, which it sabotaged with false starts—the apex type of mistake, along with delay of game, for a team about to get torched on sports radio for being "undisciplined." Another series ended when the team ran a fourth-down play toward the side of the line where Penn State already had most of its guys lined up. It was tense.

The game was kept competitive by PSU's own ineptitude—a fake field goal play that went backward, linemen not being able to decide who to block such that no one got blocked at all, and so forth. The collective creative mind of the internet has determined that Penn State coach James Franklin has an alter ego named "Frames Janklin," who makes terrible decisions during games and cannot organize his offensive players; the Nittany Lion quarterback of the past several years, Sean Clifford, is an outstanding athlete and spirited competitor but is mostly known to neutral fans as someone who is frequently seen running in the wrong direction to try to avoid a sack before fumbling. Frames coached the first half to a draw, with Clifford fumbling twice.

In the third quarter, Michigan's offense calmed down, and its overall quality advantage proved itself. Penn State jammed up the middle of the line of scrimmage, but Hassan Haskins's runs to the outside were finding open space, with each gain made marginally longer, as 247Sports writer Zach Shaw observed, because of his determination to run toward and through every attempted tackle "like it was a question of his character." (Haskins has a background similar to Ronnie Bell's—he is from Eureka, Missouri, and was only the 975th-ranked prospect in his high school class, considered too slow to play at a high level.) Michigan took a 14-6 lead. Back in New Jersey, our neighbors had come over to drink beers and eat "Rippin' Chicken Strips" from a restaurant that caters to local college students. Everything was going great.

Penn State, however, then scored to tie the game on a drive on which it picked up two fourth downs, a fourth and goal, and a two-point conversion, the latter two on closely contested catches that demonstrated either great skill and concentration or galactically disgusting luck, depending on your perspective. When Michigan got the ball back, its offensive line gave up the most direct and unencumbered sack it would give up all year, and McNamara fumbled when he got hit. At that moment, the most obviously likely outcome was that Penn State was going to score another touchdown, and Michigan would lose. It was where game momentum and overall destiny were headed. I didn't feel tense anymore, but only because the life force had left my body completely. I was on the corner of the couch with the despairing weight of another contentious off-season on top of me. Now our neighbors' presence was making me angry. Stupid neighbors! How was I supposed to be expected to talk to someone after this? It was going to ruin my day, and the next day, at the least.

Before the season, I had spoken about such moments with Chas DiCapua, the resident teacher at the Insight Meditation Society in Barre, Massachusetts. According to his biography, he has been "practicing mindfulness and Buddhist meditation, primarily in the Theravada school, for over 25 years including over two years of combined time in silent, intensive retreat." DiCapua has "trained with Burmese meditation masters, western monastics of the Thai Forest tradition and senior western Vipassana teachers," and I believe I am the first person to come to him to ask about what someone should do if they are struggling with college football.

"In terms of Buddhist understanding, the mind likes highs and lows. It doesn't like evenness. It doesn't like neutral. It likes positive, and it even prefers unpleasant over neutral, interestingly enough," he said, defining the nature of the problem. This made me think of the compulsion to look at one's phone or computer, during what would otherwise be moments of neutral boredom during the off season, to monitor the conversations and news and buzz around the team. "It's just the perfect distraction from being in the present moment," he said. "It can be interesting at those times, if we have the awareness, right when we feel ourselves wanting to check, to look and see, to say, 'What's happening right now, what's going on right now that I'm not wanting to be with?'"

He was describing mindfulness, which he recommended applying to the entirety of fandom:

> I think it's important to really take a real, honest look at, "What is it actually like when I go to watch football games?" What is that really like—seeing what the actual experience is like, not the thought in the mind of what the experience is going to be like? There's an idea in the mind, like, "Oh, good, home game this Saturday," when the mind touches that in a very superficial way. Home game Saturday equals good. Get down below that. What's actually happening? Okay, it took two hours to get to the parking lot. And after the game, it took an hour to get out of the

parking lot, and it took two hours to drive home. You just pay close, close, close attention. What's actually happening during the game? How's my body? Is it relaxed, or is it completely contracted and uptight? Even when your team is ahead like thirty to nothing, the other team gets the ball and starts to drive, and it's like, "Oh, no. The tide's going to change. Oh, no, we might lose." Understanding that there's no rest. One always has to be tense.

I had been trying to take his advice about self-examination over the course of the season, most notably during the unexpectedly close Rutgers game, during which I noticed myself thinking, "This sucks," "Why can't they run the ball all of a sudden?" and "I don't like this."

It is DiCapua's belief that being aware of such feelings will naturally allow for the improvement of one's mindset. "It's not about dropping it: 'I will not go to football games anymore,'" he said. "It's not willful. Pay close attention: Is it serving you? Is it serving your happiness? And if not, then we let it go, not because it's wrong or bad but because we want to be at ease, we want to be happy. And when we see clearly something's getting in the way of that, then it kind of naturally lets go, like ripe fruit falling from a tree."

He wasn't saying anyone *should* give up watching sports, only that they would end up doing it upon introspection if it really were destructive to them. But giving up the habit intentionally is something most fans with an emotional attachment to one or more teams have thought about as a matter of self-protection. There are also ethical reasons to consider doing so, of which the Robert Anderson sexual abuse scandal was Michigan's most egregious example.

Anderson was the University of Michigan doctor who was affiliated with the university for thirty-seven years and was accused by more than a thousand people of sexual misconduct. There has been an unbecoming reluctance in some quarters to reconsider Bo Schembechler, who is accused of being one of Anderson's enablers. Radio play-by-play announcer Jim Brandstatter, a former player who has long been officially affiliated with the program, speculated in June 2021 that the individuals who'd said they told Schembechler about misconduct may have had "compensatory, monetary" motivations. ("I'm just saying, that's a question that should be asked," he said, and then he argued that as an evidentiary matter, his convictions about Schembechler's character should "carry as much weight as his accusers," who are speaking about things they say they experienced personally.) Jim Harbaugh said in the same month that "the Bo Schembechler I know" would not have "sat on anything."

Ultimately, absolving Schembechler of responsibility is a way to absolve oneself. If he was given a good idea that abuse was taking place and blew it off because he didn't think doing something about it was as important as winning at football, that's not only on him but also on everyone whose aggregate obsession with a game put him in a position to feel that such a decision was justified.

College fandom has also long supported a system of distributing revenue that, whatever one wants to say about its intentions, creates outcomes that are absurdly and even tragically unfair. The head coaches who would've lost nearly all their games if not for Denard Robinson are set with generational wealth, while Robinson's entire four-year NFL career earned him about as much in total as what they made each season. Hall of Fame Michigan basketball player Chris Webber, of the early '90s "Fab Five," was banned for years from being around the university for accepting money from a booster named Ed Martin (who is, come to think of it, the only person I've ever seen referred to as a Michigan booster rather than a Michigan donor). While it would be hard to quantify, you cannot convince me that the entire athletic program is not still to some extent coasting (and making money) off the energy and mystique that Webber created as the best player on those unforgettable teams.

I thought about what it would be like to exist as not-a-football-fan. Who would I be? How would I think of myself? "Well, I mean, from a Buddhist perspective, there is no self," DiCapua said. "But how to articulate who you are, it's more like a verb than a noun. Who we are is emotion. We are the angry one we were this morning or the kind one we were this afternoon. We can articulate ourselves much more in the moment, rather than some aesthetic idea that doesn't change, because who we are is constantly changing in both body and mind and heart. We would describe ourselves as something much more fluid than I am a this or I am a that." Hmm.

"If people don't have something that is meaningful to them, really deeply meaningful, then the absence of that is a big hole," DiCapua said. "And guess what we try to fill it with? Great experiences. [If] we're not connected to something larger than ourselves spiritually, then, well, let's connect to something larger than ourselves in being a fan of a particular team. We end up demanding a lot out of that experience." Well, he had me there.

———◆———

Not having a fixed self, however, seemed like it would be a bummer. I had spoken about that issue with Erin Tarver, the Emory University philosophy professor with an expertise in sports and pop culture. Philosophers are widely understood to have thought deeply about whether things are good or bad, so I thought she might be able to provide guidance about whether the urge toward belonging, and the specific kind of geographic and personal-origin belonging that college football highlights, had a positive worth that could justify the significant trade-offs. "Is it okay to want to be from somewhere?" I had asked. "Is that a human good, or just what people do because they're kind of wired to?" Tarver responded,

> I think some people are rightly very worried about that. Designating a "we versus they" or "us versus them," in the course of human history, has turned out quite badly. It tends to foster feelings of loyalty and narcissism that are dangerous and dehumanizing of other groups. But I don't think it's of necessity a bad thing to mark out an "us and them," because I think it's part of how we become selves in the world. This is part of what it is to become a person. It is dangerous, and it can be and has been used for all kinds of nefarious purposes. But I don't think that the act of saying "me" or the act of having allegiance to one group over another is inherently suspect. Families do the same thing. We aren't isolated atoms in our becoming individuals. So the ability to be able to recognize a certain community as ours, I think, is quite important from a psychological perspective, and from the perspective of having a meaningful human life.

Elsewhere, Tarver has written about "the pleasure of knowing and feeling ourselves as a group, and being called to collective engagement that makes us significant in ways beyond what any one of us could ever hope to attain individually," as well as "the affirmation of one's selfhood as an individual belonging to a community that matters." That hits it on the head. Of course, what follows after the second phrase I quoted is a caveat that the same urges cause wars.

I had read a related book called *We Average Unbeautiful Watchers* by a professor at Washington University in St. Louis named Noah Cohan. The book is about sports fandom as depicted in books and movies and carried out online on personal blogs. (Its title is a reference to an article that David Foster Wallace wrote about Roger Federer, and it was written in the mid-aughts, when blogs were big.) Cohan's premise is that, contra the self-deprecating ideas about "caring about a game being played by people you don't even know" or "rooting for laundry," there is nothing more intrinsically trivial about finding dramatic or emotional satisfaction in sports than there is in finding it in, say, a story in a novel or on a TV show or in a play by Shakespeare. Why should there be anything more respectable about crying at the opera than reacting emotionally to a football team? I have seen a few operas, and frankly, they are ridiculous. The end of an opera is always something like a woman swallowing a poison sword because her boyfriend, who is also a dragon, has been cast out of his kingdom by a witch who stole a magic harp. At least a football game actually happened! *Swan Lake* isn't real!

Writes Cohan, "While sports fandom may look or even feel akin to madness, like our connection to literature such fandom allows us to build identities on the firm footing of established communal narratives without denying the interpretive flexibility borne of our own idiosyncrasies." In layperson's terms, games, seasons, and careers create stories about people and conflict. Like a well-known ancient myth or *The Godfather,* they allow us to have common reference points with other people who are trying to understand how the world works and how humans act in different situations. But they can also have specific relevance in our own lives because who we were with when they took place, or where we lived, or what else was going on in the world at large or our part of it. They happen to everyone at once but also to everyone on their own. And in some cases—like the creation of sabermetrics among baseball fans leading to the regime of Billy Beane and to *Moneyball*, and from there to a broad change in the way Major League hitters think about drawing walks—the way that these stories are collectively interpreted actually interacts with the sport itself. Sports outcomes are objective, but everyone participates in deciding what they really mean.

In his discussion of *A Fan's Notes*—a fictionalized memoir published in 1968 by a writer named Frederick Exley, who depicts his New York Giants fanaticism in context of his alcoholism, mental illness, and general obnoxiousness—Cohan touches on a related subject, which is the idea that it's embarrassing to be concerned about something that isn't rational and tangible. The assumption is inherent in many sports fans' most self-critical impulses. But Cohan asks, What kind of person would Exley be if his attachment to the Giants could be lobotomized out of him? The idea of extinguishing the emotional response to sports seems appealing in moments like the nadir of the Penn State game, but being someone who only cares about events in which they are directly involved, in which their self-interest can be quantified, would be an impoverished way to move through life. (To be clear, as Cohan emphasized when we spoke on the phone, "If sports fandom is not working for you, if it makes you an alcoholic or whatever, please give it up.")

The intrinsicness of all this was on display in my own house, in the person of my five-year-old son. Conscious of my own fandom extremes and the history of overbearing sports dads, I have been careful not to suggest to him that he should play or be a fan of any particular sport or team. He has, nonetheless, been very strongly drawn to, among other things, baseball, soccer, and the Cincinnati Bengals (the NFL team nearest to where my in-laws live). He demands to see highlight shows and runs back and forth reenacting the plays being shown. (I've been careful not to exclude my oldest daughter from sports activity, but she usually declines invitations to hit or kick a ball so she can continue conspiring, often in a corner, with her imaginary friends "Shyla" and "Jarro." Interesting kid.)

My son's behaviors are modulated little if at all by social concerns or "performance" of the kind that Goffman writes about. Many of his sports attachments developed during the initial phase of the pandemic, when he wasn't socializing with anyone at all outside his family. He merely thinks what athletes are doing is amazing and cool, and his brain is wired to want to find out who wins and who loses. (There is a reason, as others have pointed out, why religions and countries explain themselves in terms of stories about the successes and failures of individual people.)

In 1972, a sociologist named Clifford Geertz published an article about the culture around the sport of cockfighting on the Indonesian island of Bali. In the course of that article, he quotes a Canadian literary critic named Northrop Frye talking about *Macbeth* and Charles Dickens. I apologize for the layers of Literary Person names that are appearing here and assure you that I know nothing about Northrop Frye besides this quotation, have not read *Macbeth* since my seventh-grade English teacher distributed what I assume was an abridged version of it, and associate Dickens primarily with *The Muppet Christmas Carol.* But the quote has become essential to my understanding: "You wouldn't go to *Macbeth* to learn about the history of Scotland—you go to it to learn what a man feels like after he's gained a kingdom and lost his soul. When you meet such a character as Micawber in Dickens, you don't feel that there must have been a man Dickens knew who was exactly like this: you feel that there's a bit of Micawber in almost everybody you know, including yourself."

Geertz relates this to cockfighting, but also really to every sport that people play, watch, and talk about: "Balinese go to cockfights to find out what a man, usually composed, aloof, almost obsessively self-absorbed, a kind of moral autocosm, feels like when, attacked, tormented, challenged, insulted, and driven in result to the extremes of fury, he has totally triumphed or been brought totally low."

Tarver and Cohan make a case that this kind of sports-related belonging and life processing has value. The problem arises when its benefits are permitted to transcend concern for the well-being of the people actually playing. In other words, like DiCapua said, you have to pay attention, and not just to what's happening during the game.

During our conversation, DiCapua mentioned that he'd once watched the New England Patriots play every week. It was evident he'd been a football fan of some sort from the accuracy with which he described the creeping terror of an opponent beginning a comeback. I asked him if that habit had indeed fallen away in his meditative years, like ripe fruit. Did he still feel compelled to see each game? "Not so much," he said, laughing. But then he clarified. "If they're in the playoffs," he said, "I'll watch that." Go Blue, but mindfully.

———◆———

The darndest thing happened after McNamara's fumble on the sixteen-yard line. On first down, Penn State gained three yards. On second down, Clifford (Sean Clifford, not Clifford Geertz) was forced into an incomplete throw because Ojabo, Hutchinson, and nose tackle Mazi Smith were about to converge on him for a three-man sack. On third down, Michigan deployed a delectable defensive ruse in which lineman Mike Morris lined up over the football as if to rush the passer but then ran back after the snap to cover Penn State's tight end. Penn State's running back, who was responsible for blocking any extra pass rushers, took a wrong step toward the middle of the line where Morris had been while Brad Hawkins, the safety, tore in toward Clifford from the outside. With Hawkins incoming, the quarterback threw off his back foot, and his pass landed several yards away from its intended receiver. Penn State, having only gained three yards with this golden scoring opportunity, had to kick a field goal, putting them ahead 17-14.

With six minutes now remaining, Michigan got the ball and gave it to Haskins four times in a row, gaining two first downs. Then he had another carry that gained one yard, creating a second and nine at Penn State's forty-seven-yard line. On the play,

Michigan lined up with three receivers to McNamara's right. They ran routes across the field from right to left. From the left side of the line, Erick All stepped out and ran to the right. The Penn State player following All collided with one of his teammates, who was crossing the other way, leaving All wide open for one of McNamara's highly effective short throws. He caught the ball and turned toward the end zone. On my couch in New Jersey, I sat up, excited by the green space I saw in front of him but unwilling to say anything aloud until the play was safely over. Instead, I pointed at the screen and made grunting noises in the direction of my wife and neighbors. All kept on running all the way down the sideline. He was met at the one-yard line by a Penn State safety, but it was too late. He toppled over into the end zone with the ball. Touchdown, Michigan, 21-17.

The Nittany Lions did not score again. When they got the ball back, they couldn't get a first down. On fourth and two with the game on the line, they tried a crossing-route play like the one that had gotten All open, but two Michigan linemen, including, once again, the confounding and enigmatic Mike Morris, dropped back and hit the crossing receivers. Morris clobbered his guy, knocking him over. The hit, in this circumstance, may have run afoul of rules regarding defensive holding and contact with receivers away from the play. In any case, Clifford threw deep left in a panic toward someone else, the pass was incomplete, and no flags were thrown, so the matter is closed. There is no need to get all litigious in criticizing the decisions made by referees in Michigan games after the fact.

The postgame mood in the Pennsylvania hills was very upbeat. While answering a press conference question about Michigan's pass rush, Harbaugh digressed into praising the offense but then paused. "How about those Wolverines?" he said. "If that's not great, I don't know what is!" He also told the media about Daylen Baldwin and his pants being on fire. Later, the team posted a video of him speaking to the team in the locker room. "You were born for this," he said. "You guys were born for days like this."

Weren't we all? *Erick All's long sideline run*, I mused to myself. *Erick All's sideline run into history. Erick All's long sideline run through the gathering darkness of . . .* and so on. But I became concerned that if the story got out of control, got too powerful, it could convince me that Michigan might beat Ohio State. And that, as a matter of metaphysical certainty, was never going to happen!

INTERLUDE

Jim Harbaugh, describing the Michigan–Penn State game on the Monday after it was played:

There was a winner, there was a nonwinner. But the real winner was football.

CHAPTER

11

OHIO STATE

If the locomotive of the Lord runs us down,
we should give thanks that the end had magnitude.

—Jack Gilbert, "A Brief for the Defense"

"WHAT WOULD YOU EVEN DO if they won?" This was my mother-in-law, who was once again preparing to help watch my children while I drove to Ann Arbor to visit friends and go to a football game. She was asking about Michigan beating Ohio State in the final game of the regular season. It's a matchup that, for Michigan, is almost always more important than anything that happens afterward in a bowl game. This was especially true this year, since a victory would also likely mean winning the Big Ten. Strategically, I refused to consider the possibility aloud.

Everywhere I went, my friends and my enemies alike were reminding me that Michigan would probably lose. "It's going to be a bloodbath," someone said in the email chain. A video was circulating that portrayed Michigan, vis-à-vis Ohio State, as the underdog Rebel Alliance from the Star Wars series. Justin, a non-aligned fan who was coming to the game with me and my friend Tim (best known for sitting with me in East Lansing in Chapter 7), said that a better analogy for Michigan would be the Mitt Romney presidential campaign, which made me mad because it was very funny and very true. Most underdogs aren't sitting on a cool $17 billion. It also meant, as an analogy, that Michigan was going to lose.

The near-term cause of the "bloodbath" comment was that the previous week, Ohio State had beaten Michigan State 56-7. And of course Michigan State had earlier beaten Michigan by four. Basic math indicated that Michigan was going to lose to the Buckeyes by fifty-three points.

The Wolverines had moreover achieved one (1.000) victory against Ohio State since 2003. The lone win was registered in 2011, a weird season in which OSU was playing with an interim coach because of one of its many cheating scandals. That was fifteen losses in sixteen games. Michigan lost to Ohio State for every reason and suffered every kind of football misfortune, from its quarterbacks being injured before the game to its quarterbacks being injured during the game, to controversial (i.e., deeply incorrect) referee decisions to, in 2019, Ohio State's running back fumbling the ball in a potentially pivotal situation in the first quarter only for the ball to bounce back directly into his hands such that he didn't even have to break his stride. It was a huge buildup and a new, different kind of huge letdown every year. I remember feeling so downtrodden in 2007 about the four straight losses at that point. It was so heartbreaking and unfair to have to go that long without a ray of sunshine, I felt. But now 2007 was a thousand years and a thousand defeats ago. It felt both farcical and cruel to be on the end of that streak—and somehow pointed and personal. I mean, it's ridiculous! When else has something like this happened? And why did it have to happen to us?

Admittedly, the biggest reason Michigan lost was competitive inferiority. Ohio State had been the higher-ranked team in all but three of those sixteen games, which basically meant that Michigan could only reasonably have expected to win three times instead of once. Bad luck was part of the problem, but not all of it.

Ohio State built its advantage a number of ways. In the early years of the streak, when Michigan's coach was Lloyd Carr and Ohio State's coach was Jim Tressel, the teams were mostly equal in talent, and the Buckeyes basically just played better. Tressel was a stern-looking, hard-ass kind of coach who enjoyed running the ball, exchanging punts, and winning 14-3 if possible (the score of the 2007 Michigan–Ohio State game), but he also adapted earlier than Carr to the possibility of having a running quarterback, putting four wide receivers on the field at the same time, and winning games 42-39 (the score of the 2006 Michigan–Ohio State game).

After Carr retired and Ohio State grudgingly replaced Tressel because he'd attested falsely in a document to not knowing whether his players had received "impermissible benefits" (free stuff from local businesses), the differences between the programs gets easier to explain: Michigan hired Rich Rodriguez and Brady Hoke (sad trombone) while Ohio State hired Urban Meyer (triumphant bugle), who is one of the two or three most successful modern-era college football coaches and was available because he'd quit his job at Florida just a year earlier, citing a desire to focus on his health and family, which evidently were no longer concerns after twelve months.

At Florida and OSU, Meyer was at the forefront of the spread-offense trend, with the distinguishing trait that he liked to have heavier quarterbacks and running backs who could run inside when the defense became too concerned about the faster guys hovering on the periphery. As Bud Elliott mentioned, Ohio State was able to trampoline off its upward-trending success with Meyer right as digital film took off, and as the College Football Playoff put a spotlight on the best teams, to become a major recruiting player in the South, particularly in Texas. Michigan was not able to do those things.

As alluded to earlier, there was also a certain amount of corner cutting—or what Michigan would call corner cutting—at Ohio State. In my mind, this is represented by the team's star late-'90s linebacker Andy Katzenmoyer, who in 1998 took one course in golf and one called "AIDS: What Every College Student Should Know" during summer school to remain academically eligible. In the present day, the team's players sometimes take classes online so they can stay in the football facilities as much as possible. The program's most recent GSR of 81 percent is the second lowest in the Big Ten, and before that it was the lowest in the conference (in the sixties, which would be low even in the SEC) for four straight years.

The "impermissible benefits" scandal that knocked Tressel out was his second. Thanks to legislation and litigation, the rules of college football now allow players to be compensated. But few if any coaches advocated for this change, and it is reasonable to suspect that some of them, hypothetically, might have previously approved the surreptitious distribution of financial benefits not as a matter of economic justice but because it was useful for player recruiting and retention. Ohio State always denied any such motivation and disavowed the players involved, expressing disappointment at what they had done. Replacing Tressel with Meyer was also a questionable move, integrity-wise, as his subsequent career has shown. (In 2018, he was suspended for three games after revelations that he had failed to act on multiple domestic violence allegations against a longtime assistant. He left OSU after that season.

In 2021, he was hired to coach the NFL's Jacksonville Jaguars but was fired before the season ended after a number of incidents and alleged incidents that demonstrated poor personal judgment.)

I don't hold the behavior of Ohio State's administrators and past coaches against its players, though. Many of them have been infuriatingly deserving of their success, most prominently, in 2021, a group of skinny wide receivers—Chris Olave, Garrett Wilson, and Jaxon Smith-Njigba—who are all ridiculously fast, elusive, and possessing of dexterous hands with impossible tensile strength, superhuman concentration and agility, and Olympian leaping ability. The current coaching regime is led by a guy named Ryan Day, who seems fine. He's a generic smart guy with a beard who used to work for Chip Kelly, the Oregon visionary, and seems like he would probably have a job in finance or technology if he didn't coach football.

It felt like winter started on the drive from southern Ohio to Ann Arbor the Friday afternoon before the game. The farther north I went, the more snow and ice was along the road. I stopped in Bowling Green, Ohio, less than thirty miles from the border, for gas and because there was a Starbucks there. It was cold. The air was still. There were cheerleaders in the Starbucks—Bowling Green University is a Mid-American Conference school and had played earlier in the day in its stadium across the street. The cheerleaders were wearing an Antarctic number of layers. I would not have gone to see a 3-8 Bowling Green team play a football game in that temperature for anything less than $50,000.

I got back in the car and on the interstate. I was fired up from listening to rap music that was popular before I got old and had repeatedly mentally rehearsed the reasons that Michigan had a chance to win. At 10-1 with only the one narrow loss, it was probably the best Michigan team that had a home game against Ohio State since the losing streak had started. (The other standout teams—2006, 2016, 2018—had played in Columbus.) Ohio State was 10-1 too and favored by nearly a touchdown, but its defense had been suspect in a number of games. Every lever that Harbaugh had pulled on the coaching-staff slot machine had come up as a winner. The strategic changes he'd made, which at Michigan had always seemed like they were a year or two too late, were clicking. And if these were going to be the players that broke through, they deserved it after crawling to freedom through five hundred yards of shit-smelling foulness (the 2020 season).

I felt nerves circulating and pressing outward in my stomach and chest, an immanent sense of dramatic apocalypse, a foreboding of the final war between the gods, and an intangible spiritual conviction that I was fated to conclude a journey of many years and leap miles into the sky in a single instant. Simply put, I had consumed too much caffeine.

———— ◆ ————

Players like the bright lights. It is not necessarily a drawback for them to play somewhere where fans care to the point of having existential mental blowouts. Ryan Clark mentioned this when he told me about choosing LSU. "You're packing up to go to a hotel for home games, and you already see people outside cooking, drinking," he said. (Teams spend the night before the game at a hotel, even at home, for what I presume are curfew reasons.) "It just felt good to feel important, to feel like what you did mattered."

"The price of being at a school like Michigan," former offensive tackle and team staffer Grant Newsome said—by which he meant one of the biggest-time schools there is—"is people are invested in you." (He's since been promoted to tight ends coach.) He even interpreted the traveling cloud of angst and complaining around the team as a positive thing. "It's natural, because they feel invested in it, and that's part of being passionate about something, is that it affects you like that. You understand that, even when there's criticism, it's coming from a place of people being invested. And there's a lot of people who I'm sure wouldn't say they're Michigan fans but seem to be invested in Michigan football too." By that he meant the haters. "That's the price you pay. Everyone wants to have an opinion about you."

On the Saturday Michigan played Ohio State, the bright lights were on, literally, because the sky was so gray and filled with swirling snow that illumination was needed even though it was a noon game. I was going through the same gate I had used for the first game of the year, against Western Michigan, and the lines to get in were about twenty times as long. The people of Michigan football weren't admitting it, but they were ready for something big to happen. "I've been covering Michigan–Ohio State games for several decades," tweeted Bob Wojnowski, who has worked for the Detroit News since 1989. "I have never seen more people outside the stadium, clogging the streets, jamming the sidewalks, in my life."

I was staring upward at the top of a pine tree next to the stadium that must be fifty or sixty feet tall, watching the snow fall past the set of lights behind it, spacing out a bit. "If we win this game, I may never see another day," said someone behind us. From the vantage of our tailgate, I had counted thirty-eight Michigan flags flying alongside and above rows of vehicles that stretched away from the stadium in lines a half mile long. Before walking to the game, the five of us who were going in together turned on the car and sat inside for several minutes to conserve warmth. Through trial and error, moving them around from my hat to inside my socks and such, I had figured out that the best way to use hand warmers is to tape them directly to your stomach. The package specifically warns you not to do this, but it means you can hunch over every few minutes and pull in your extremities so that the heat radiates to every part of your body.

Tim and I were seated about eighty rows up above the corner of one of the end zones. Our other three friends (including Justin, the hater) were using a different set of tickets somewhere else. Behind us was a row of young OSU fans who had a wine-bar vibe to them. To our left was a guy who was wearing a full Michigan football uniform, including a helmet, shoulder pads, and thigh pads—truly everything that's part of a uniform—that appeared to be homemade. It made it a pain to get out of his way when he went to the bathroom, but it gave our row a seriousness of purpose. You probably don't see that guy at a wine bar very often. This was really the main event, for him.

The game began with Michigan receiving the ball and driving down the field mostly by having Haskins thunder through the middle. Michigan scored a touchdown when McNamara faked a throw to five-star freshman Donovan Edwards to his left and handed off behind his back to A. J. Henning, the team's smallest and zippiest player, for an end-around to the right. This was the kind of balance the team had been trying for years to get right: tricky "spread" stuff set up by the legitimate threat of old-fashioned brutality inside.

When Ohio State got the ball, its players were thrown off by the volubility of the crowd. Michigan Stadium can be sedate sometimes because of its open bowl layout and genteel clientele, but on this day, everyone in attendance was standing from beginning to end. There was an edge to it. The Buckeyes' kick returner bungled the kick, so OSU started on its four-yard line. Then its center snapped the ball to quarterback C. J. Stroud when he wasn't ready; Stroud was luckily able to fall on it. OSU had to punt, and Michigan advanced on a quick strike to receiver Roman Wilson. Everything was going very, very well. Then, in a play that seemed to happen in a microsecond, McNamara dropped back and threw toward Wilson again for what would have been a touchdown that put OSU in a stunned 14-0 hole. But an OSU safety had figured out the play and cut over decisively to intercept it. Whoosh. The exact kind of letting-them-off-the-hook mistake Michigan had made in this series so many times. Frhh-ghhjfhfh. Fww;dsflkjdlfkj!!

"It's over," said one of the younger, male OSU fans behind us, implying, I assumed, that the interception would deflate Michigan mentally and allow Ohio State's talent to exert its inexorable advantage. And indeed, for the next hour and a half, the game went back and forth like normal games do, with most of us working under the expectation that Michigan was eventually going to lose. But I think the interception and the modest success Ohio State subsequently achieved mostly made the actual Michigan players mad. When OSU scored to take the lead (on an incredible twisting leaping catch by Wilson at the end zone pylon) in the second quarter, Michigan scored in response on an eighty-two-yard drive. On fourth and one at OSU's forty-three-yard line, the right side of Michigan's offensive line casually pushed the Buckeyes' hotshot defenders back two yards as Haskins ran behind them. McNamara then dropped a ball to receiver Cornelius Johnson inside the five-yard line. Johnson skidded about twenty feet after hitting the ground on the wet field, which was glittering as if covered in tinsel for most of the day because of the snow. Then Haskins scored.

No one in the stadium knew it at the time, but the course of the rest of the game was set when the teams went into the tunnel to the locker room at halftime. Former OSU quarterback and current *GameDay* host Kirk Herbstreit was there and posted a video of it. Ohio State passes by first and looks like a team of football players walking to their locker room. Not dejected or arguing with each other, just guys doing one of the boring things you do in life between the interesting things. Behind them, though, you can hear a wall of hooting and shouting. Then the Michigan team comes into view, pressed up against the referees, who are holding the line between the teams. Every player on Michigan is gesturing toward the Buckeyes and engaged in . . . what? Boisterous catcalling, let's say, a reminder that they were there and not going away. The looks on the Ohio State players' faces as they turn back toward the noise convey something along the lines of, *What is happening? What is this?*

When the teams came back out for the second half, Ohio State ran the ball three times in a row, but on third down and two, its blockers were stalemated by Michigan's defensive line while senior linebacker Josh Ross (whose older brother had played the same position at Michigan seven years earlier) swooped in, slipped sideways between linemen, and tackled the Buckeyes' TreVeyon Henderson for a loss. Ohio State punted and then Michigan ran three times for a total of eighty-one yards and a touchdown. Haskins scored from thirteen yards out on a sweep behind Erick All that was so well set up as a play call that I turned away to celebrate about three seconds before it was over. Haskins held All's jersey from behind while they ran into the end zone, like a kid following their dad through the mall. 21-13.

The ball went back to Ohio State, and its line was called for a holding penalty and a false start and then allowed a third-down sack to Aidan Hutchinson, who bounced off the field with his left hand in the air in a fist. Michigan ball. This time the Wolverines advanced by faking handoffs and passing deep—a thirty-one-yard dime by McCarthy to Wilson and a thirty-four-yard flea-flicker by McNamara to a delightfully wide-open Sainristil. (One of the fun things about seeing games in person is being able to see where a pass is headed the entire time it's in the air. Guys are very open quite frequently. Covering the whole field is hard!) The crowd in the other corner of the stadium exploded after the next play, a short run, and there was pushing and shoving on the far side of the field. No one on our side had seen it, but an OSU defensive back, Cameron Brown, had ripped Wilson's helmet off and away from the play after Wilson goaded him by grabbing his leg from the ground. Two Michigan offensive linemen came in hot and went face-to-face with Brown. A scrum developed, into which All appeared like a lightning bolt. A penalty was called on Brown, but the ball was already on the one-yard line. On the next play, Haskins scored again, running left. All, his bodyguard, had the lead block, meeting his man on the outside at the line of scrimmage and knocking him a yard deep in the end zone. 28-13.

The crowd was getting giddy. Michigan was on a roll where every other play was the kind of major strike that you sometimes go entire games (or seasons!) without seeing. This—winning—was possibly actually happening. It was too cold to hold a pen to take notes, but I remember that I kept crouching, turning, and punching Tim squarely in the chest, that being the form that my disbelief and excitement was taking. There was, for some reason, a DJ on Michigan's sideline who was being shown on the video screen, and he kept playing a pounding, repetitive Belgian techno song called "Pump It Up" about how "you got to pump it up." At first, this seemed very random. (It turns out the players had been listening to it while lifting weights.) Then it became hypnotizing. Then it became the rhythm of an entire army, its weird mechanical European heart beating as one with ours.

Months after the fact, I consulted two experts on Xs and Os, one on each side of the rivalry—for Ohio State, *Columbus Dispatch* writer Bill Rabinowitz, and for Michigan, a guy who goes by the name "Space Coyote" on Twitter. (He's legit!) I asked them in essence if it would be too simple to attribute the game outcome to Michigan's players, particularly on the defensive and offensive lines, "wanting it more" than Ohio State's. Mr. Coyote noted that Michigan's secondary kept switching which players it used to double-team Olave and Wilson, which may have thrown off Stroud's timing. He also thought that Michigan had prepared well to run the ball in ways that messed with the Buckeyes' typical defensive assignments. (Rewatching some of the highlights, you can see Ohio State's linebackers running the wrong way a lot, expecting the play to go outside when it's going inside and such.) Rabinowitz observed that penalties often put the Buckeyes in situations where they couldn't afford to risk long pass attempts—the kinds of plays they'd destroyed Michigan State with the previous week and destroyed Michigan with in the teams' last two games—because they had to prioritize getting a first down.

Michigan's guys also did beat the guys across from them. Stroud didn't have time to wait for his eel-like receivers to find open space because Hutchinson and Ojabo were right there on him every time, and Henderson never had room to run at all. On offense, having a plan is nice, but carrying it out still requires everyone to do their job, which Michigan's guys did. This was a triumph of the underdog in at least some sense: on the whole, Ohio State had better recruits on its team. This is not exactly the same as having better players, but it's close. The penalties and the assignment confusion, moreover, seem likely to have been at least in some part a function of OSU's players having underestimated the zeal that both their opponent and their opponent's crowd would bring to the contest.

The fourth quarter was spent in suspense waiting for a climactic moment that Ohio State was not eager to allow. Its offense scored two touchdowns on drives that were, under the circumstances, heroic. Stroud and his receivers were too good to completely stop; twice, on a third and nineteen and a fourth and four, the quarterback threw passes to Smith-Njigba that the latter caught despite approximately 97 percent of the surface area of his body being completely occluded by a Michigan defender. After the first OSU touchdown, however, Michigan scored in response on a drive during which it ran the ball eight times. It took OSU four and a half minutes of game time to score again, completing the drive by throwing a fourth and goal pass to Henderson over the fingertips of a leaping Hutchinson, who, if he had been able to intercept the ball, would have had an outside chance at returning it ninety yards for a touchdown depending on how the blocking shook out. It's maybe good that that didn't happen, because the reaction may have caused the fissile combustion of Michigan Stadium and the entire Earth. But it felt a teensy bit at the time like the "game of inches" moment we might look back on as the beginning of another nauseating unraveling.

It wasn't. After the kickoff, Haskins ran for two first downs. On the second, he gained seven yards after being hit by the guy who tackled him—the country strength of Eureka, Missouri, in action. With 2:25 on the clock, he took another handoff at Ohio State's thirty-one-yard line for what instantly became one of the defining plays of the 130-year history of Michigan football. Ohio State blitzed to the right side of Michigan's line, but the play was set up to go the other way. Haskins hit a huge hole created when left tackle Ryan Hayes (335th nationally in his recruiting class) threw defensive end Zach Harrison (12th nationally in his recruiting class) onto the ground, cut left toward the end zone to open field, slapped away a safety's hand at the twenty-yard line, met an OSU cornerback who was lowering himself for a tackle attempt at the eight-yard line, *leaped over him*, and kept running, a clean hurdle. At this moment on the recording of Fox's broadcast, the pitch of the crowd rises into the stratosphere and seems to blow out the network's microphones for half a second. You can hear someone literally scream in disbelief. Haskins went out of bounds at the four but scored on the next play. It was his fifth touchdown of the day. Michigan led 42-27.

This might actually be it, I and everyone else realized. Ohio State only had two minutes left and trailed by two scores. Stroud threw a sixteen-yard pass on the next series, which I have no memory of at all, but I do remember that the Buckeyes then had the ball at around midfield with just over a minute left on a third down and that Stroud dropped back, tried to run away to his right, and got tracked down and sacked by a rampant and unstoppable

Ojabo, the Scottish Nightmare, to put them in fourth and nine-teen. On the next play, Ojabo almost got Stroud again, and Stroud had to spin and run even farther backward and to his left, finally throwing a completion to Olave. But the pass didn't go very far, and Olave was tackled immediately. I looked to the sideline at the first-down marker. It wasn't close. It was Michigan's ball, and they would be able to run out the clock without needing a first down. For some reason, I turned around, pulled off my COVID-19 mask, and started screaming at the people two rows behind us. (The OSU fans had vacated; it was wine o'clock.) "It's over, it's over," I kept saying, just to make sure it was over.

I took a video of the clock reaching zero, and the routine parts of the scene stand out, like the final score being read on the PA ("*Mee-ichigan* 42, Ohio State 27") and the marching band playing. Familiar things, but in an unfamiliar context, a sudden new world. The lower rows of the stadium emptied on to the field until it was completely full of humans, while the upper rows moved down to the lower rows. It felt less like a sporting event than the wind-down after a graduation ceremony or a wedding. There were tens of thousands of people hugging and slapping backs. Some cried. After maybe fifteen minutes, the PA announcer apologeti-cally asked everyone if they wouldn't mind letting the players off the field, and after maybe ten more minutes, he asked if everyone wouldn't mind starting to leave. Tim and I stayed around, talking about the game and soaking it in until the collective move toward the exits finally started. And that was what I did when they won.

So. What did we learn?

I learned the way a lot of fans and observers think about sports is too rigid. They operate as if any given player or, especially, any given coach is intrinsically "good" or "bad" and that you win by compiling as many "good" inputs as possible. But people fail or succeed together. The 2021 Michigan season was the result of some specific coaches making smart plans and some specific players being extremely athletic and good at football. But it was also the result of cosmic vibrations around a common belief system.

In talking to one former Michigan player who didn't want to be quoted directly about some successes and failures he had been a part of, and that he had observed in the program after he graduated, I realized he was talking about teams in the way biologists talk about an ecosystem. One thing going wrong cascades and screws up everything else, even parts of the system that would otherwise be working. Players don't need to like each other, but they need to trust each other. They have to trust that everyone else is going to work as hard in the off-season and try as hard on the field as they are. ("If a guy misses a snap count, but you know they bring it every day, they have credibility," another player said. "Versus a guy who you know is missing class, late to practice, not giving it all.") The coaches don't have to be buddies with the players, but the players need to know that the coaches are trying to help them improve themselves, help them get ready for the NFL or whatever it is they plan to do next, and aren't just looking for their own next job. Players want to understand why they're being asked to do what they're doing both on the field and in general. Take out just one of the links in this great chain, and before too long you're losing to Indiana.

Before the 2021 season, Michigan's ecosystem of trust looked, from the outside, like the site of a record-breaking oil spill. But while there may have been internal debate about results and methods, I don't believe anyone at Michigan considered changing its topline goal: having a football team whose players go to class, represent the university by being well-spoken and well-rounded and well-behaved and all that—"they actually do believe this stuff," John Bacon told me—and ending the regular season by absolutely whaling on Ohio State.

A college football coach has a recursive job: if he can persuade people his way of doing things is a winning one, it probably will be. And because of the way the US college system happens to have evolved, and the way humans value the particularities of their social and geographic groups, there are enough different ways of winning to go around. That's the beauty of the whole enterprise. I mentioned Dabo Swinney's (unofficially) Christian summer camp at Clemson earlier, though I did not mention my favorite fact about the operation, which is that (at least at one point) someone kept tallies of which recruits held doors open for the people behind them during campus visits. There's a leaked video online of Nick Saban pitching Alabama to a recruit over a video chat by reeling off a number of staggering stats about its success both as a team and as an NFL training academy, then concluding that "it's not for everyone," as if to say, Take it or leave it, bud. Lane Kiffin is always smiling and stumbling into a new feud. He would call a deep pass on every play if it were feasible. Iowa coach Kirk Ferentz personifies the phrase "taciturn grimace," and his favorite play is punting. Both of these coaches' programs won ten games in the 2021 season.

The past few years have had mixed results for the ways of doing things in Florida and Louisiana—and without suggesting that Taggart or (especially) Orgeron did not contribute to the outcomes of their own tenures at Florida State and LSU, there was poignance to their fates. I would not have expected to feel bad for either of them: both are scheduled to be paid around $15 million all told from the schools that fired them, and as Taggart has already shown, many other jobs are available. But because of the way college football works, being fired from one's dream job is a lot like being exiled. Taggart's comment at his first press conference about being the first person from a Florida State family to make it to Florida State sticks in my head. "I'm in!" he said. Not for long, though.

Michigan athletic director Warde Manuel retained Jim Harbaugh after the bad 2020 season in some sense because the program wanted to succeed with someone like Harbaugh in charge. Harbaugh's family had been around the school since 1973, when his dad had started there as an assistant coach. The question posed during the 2021 season was whether Harbaugh could persuade anyone besides Manuel of his viability.

It turned out that wasn't much of a problem. There's a misconception about Harbaugh that because he's weird and always wears the same type of pants, he must be inscrutable and antisocial. Not so. In some ways, he may be the most linear, predictable person in the world. The January 2022 off-season's main storyline turned out to be his interest in coaching in the NFL. This came as a surprise to almost everyone, but 247Sports reported that when a potential Michigan recruit's family had asked him in December whether he would consider returning to the NFL if a team contacted him, he had said directly that, yes, he would. Ultimately, he returned to Michigan, explaining in interviews that he had been drawn toward the NFL because it would give him another chance to win the Super Bowl, which he considers the pinnacle achievement in his profession. As it happened, I had recently found a November 11, 2006, article in the *San Francisco Chronicle* about his then role as University of San Diego head coach. "I've always said my dream is to coach an NFL team to the Super Bowl," he told the reporter at the time. It can be confounding to everyone who can't see inside his head, but his set of guiding beliefs are consistent.

As for social interaction, arguably the most important part of the man's job is traveling to meet parents dozens of times a year in every part of the country with the goal of creating a connection so strong that they trust him with their sons' professional development. He enjoys this. In January 2022, one of Michigan's recruits, South Carolina running back C. J. Stokes, posted a picture of Harbaugh in the Stokeses' living room in his socks. Everyone else in the picture is wearing shoes. Here's what Harbaugh later said on Michigan's in-house podcast about Stokes and another recruit, Alex Oriji:

> C. J.'s dad, Capers Stokes, I could listen to him talk all day long. The wisdom and just how he talks too. He's got that southern drawl—he grabs me. Maybe it's my age. Maybe I'm just getting to that age where you really connect with somebody, the parents and especially the dads. . . . These two guys, it's like we breathe the same air. Just the wisdom and being able to talk to those two dads is tremendous. Alex's dad, Mr. Oriji—just somebody you meet and right away—there's a lot I'm supposed to glean from this man.

He is searching for kindred spirits with whom to collaborate in the calling of football. Ben Muth said that, yes, there were people he played with who thought Harbaugh was a pain in the ass. He also said Stanford's adoption of the original "manball" running game that Harbaugh became known for was the result of a meeting he had with Stanford's offensive line after his first season, when the team's offense had been built on quick "West Coast" timing passes and other kinds of running plays. "He's like, All right, I think this is one of the better units on our team. What do we do? He literally just asked us what we wanted to run more," he said.

I spent the last year reading Jim Harbaugh press conference transcripts, and most of it was pretty boring. But there was a consistent theme—that commitment was flowing back and forth between Michigan's players and coaches. He said *committed* and *flow* a dozen times. I believe Michigan football was so successful in 2021 because it had a surplus of players who were on this wavelength, who had an obsession with football in its totality but happened to also be extremely good. (That part is important too.) Haskins, Hutchinson,

Erick All, and others were group-mission-mentality true believers. They would have been as excited as Harbaugh, their racehorse hearts going crazy, to do football drills with high school kids from New Jersey. After the Penn State game, Cade McNamara was interviewed on the field about the turn in the program's fortunes. "The class that we came in with, we wanted to be the change," he said. "We wanted to make a difference."

Fans, especially in the pessimistic corners of the internet I embedded myself in, often assume players are mercenary contractors who are one mildly adverse event away from transferring. I think that too is a misconception. As *Sports Illustrated*'s Richard Johnson had said to me, college sports "tie everybody to their youth in a way pro sports don't," and this struck me as being as true for the football players I spoke to as it is for anyone else. It's certainly possible that some players make decisions mostly based on what will maximize their individual success and exposure, but it's not always the case. Their choices account for their teammates and coaches—reasonable given the amount of time they put into a physically intense activity that requires working in very close proximity—and their families. It's a matter of both personal advancement and what kind of collective reputation they want to be a part of.

I thus came to think about Michigan's sometimes unusual way of doing things as crucial to its success. I may continue to roll my eyes about aspects of its philosophy, but I take the people who take it seriously much more seriously, if that makes sense. There was no way not to after speaking to them. Lineman Carlo Kemp said he was interested in Michigan because his mom always told him that "school always comes before sports." Receiver Donovan Peoples-Jones's mother, Roslyn, said that her son routinely beats her at *Jeopardy* and then reminds her that he has a Michigan education. (She shared this with pride.) Jarrett Irons, a linebacker and captain in the 1990s, said one reason he attended Michigan was because his grandfather, who grew up in nearby Ypsilanti, had not been able to. "I was very close to him before he passed," he said. "He always wanted to go to the University of Michigan, but he ended up going to Eastern [Michigan University], because they weren't taking African Americans. And that always sat in the back of my mind. I'd wear that winged helmet, and go to class, and I would think of my grandfather saying this was something he always wanted."

Said Irons, "Being a Michigan Man means the world to me."

———— ◆ ————

At halftime of the Ohio State game, I went out to the concourse to line up for the bathroom and saw, from the balcony, that snow had settled across the landscape from the countryside to the campus to the buildings downtown. My only reaction in the moment was getting out my phone to take a poorly framed amateur picture of it, that being the only reaction anyone has now to any stimulus. But I thought about the scene later.

Seeing the modest Ann Arbor skyline reminded me of coming to the city to visit when I was the young only child of transplanted, out-of-state ex-hippies. Our vibes as a family were not entirely aligned with the conservative-leaning, business-oriented town we lived in, you could say. (My parents have since moved to Colorado to be with the tree people.) We would visit Ann Arbor roughly once a year. We didn't go to games because the season-ticket waiting list was years long, and this was the era when the only way to scalp an extra was to pay someone in cash outside the stadium. My parents aren't the kind of people who would stake a trip that long on a transaction that uncertain. They were thrifty hippies. But at other times, we would drive there from Midland, and I would be amazed by this city where there were, among other things, hills and restaurants that were not Big Boy. There was an entire shop that sold only mystery novels, as well as a shoe store just for running shoes.

There was an enormous, all-purpose bookstore too—it was the flagship of the Borders chain, and this was when the idea of a bookstore the size of a Sears was exciting, before it was widely realized that they were putting the smaller ones out of business. (The Borders store also later went out of business.)

Ann Arbor was a point of congregation for interesting people and things—and it was relevant and important to the rest of the world. The rest of the world watched it especially closely on several Saturdays each fall.

Earlier in this book, I asked why the ardent members of the college football community are the way they are. I accounted for some causes and explanations: Thomas Jefferson's ideas about sophisticated farmers, Erving Goffman's theory of self-presentation, the economic advantages of being loud and wrong, air-conditioning, the many links between *Macbeth* and Balinese cockfighting. To make it as simple as possible, though, I think the answer is that the ardent members of the college football community are looking for a little recognition, for status, though not always even in the confrontational, competitive sense of being better than everyone else. They just want to feel, from time to time, that their way of doing things is a deserving one.

The sport has many problems. I would also prefer to be able to watch it with a greater degree of equanimity and inner peace. But—and as a journalist who covers the contemporary United States, I can say this as a factual matter—there are many problems with everything you could possibly care about. It isn't necessary to accept the things that are wrong in order to do so. I think it is beneficial to like yourself, for example, even though there are many things wrong with you. Life is a journey of never-ending conflicts and challenges, and the journey requires fuel, a hand-warmer glow to hunch over when the air turns cold. In Michigan, we saved some warmth—me, Hassan Haskins, Thicc Stauskas, everyone—on November 27, 2021. We were alive; we were together; for one day, at least, we were good. We existed. Write it on the walls of the cave: 42-27.

There is no fully explainable reason to care what happens in a game. Someday the sun will consume the Earth and with it every memory and record of Michigan and Ohio State playing football in the snow in 2021. It *doesn't* matter, in any way you can prove. But there is nothing more important.

Epilogue

Where are they now?

The Michigan football team beat Iowa 42-3 to win the Big Ten championship at a neutral-site game in Indianapolis's Lucas Oil Stadium on December 4, 2021. The game was reasonably close for a while, but Iowa ultimately proved too Iowan to keep up with the Wolverines' dynamic runners and receivers when Michigan had the ball. (I was born in Iowa, by the way.) The Hawkeyes' offense was concurrently hamstrung by Kirk Ferentz's preference for a torpid, nearly comatose pace and style. Michigan fans sang "Pump It Up" en masse and a capella, on their own initiative, during the fourth quarter. It was a beautiful December evening.

The Big Ten title was, of course, Michigan's first in seventeen years. After beating Iowa, it was ranked second in the country. The consensus among fans online was that 2021 had already been the program's best season since the national championship year of 1997. And the team was finally selected to participate in the College Football Playoff, in which it was matched up against Georgia in a national semifinal at the Orange Bowl. As you'll no doubt recall, however, the monster from the 2008 movie *Cloverfield* emerged from the Atlantic Ocean shortly before kickoff and destroyed the city of Miami, forcing the cancellation of the game, which would have likely been a comfortable Michigan win. A strange way to finish things, but it was still, all told, a good year.

Michigan State signed coach Mel Tucker to a $95 million contract extension in November, making him, at the time, the second-highest paid coach in the sport. One month before the contract was announced, the university had asked the members of its faculty to volunteer for shifts in dining halls because of staffing shortages.

Louisiana State announced after its win over Florida that Orgeron would be replaced as coach after the end of the season but continue on as an LSU athletic department employee in a vague ambassador-type role, a somewhat unusual arrangement but one that left the two parties on good terms. *Sort of* good terms. According to a subsequent report by The Athletic, the recently divorced Orgeron had behaved in ways that made others wonder whether he was properly focused on football—asking a woman at a gas station who turned out to be "the wife of a high-ranking LSU official," for instance, if she wanted to "work out" with him because she was wearing exercise clothes, then responding, "Why does that matter?" when she told him she was married. LSU then convinced Notre Dame's Brian Kelly to leave his job and accept a ten-year, $95 million contract to coach in Baton Rouge. The posters at Tiger Rant were thrilled by how articulate Kelly was during his introductory press conference. Said one, "Nice to have a guy with an IQ above room temperature and not a clown that people laugh at."

Florida Atlantic and Willie Taggart finished 5-7. The *Palm Beach Post* speculated that he may be "on the hot seat." In January 2022, ESPN wrote that his replacement at Florida State, Mike Norvell, is on the hot seat as well.

Ohio State is reaping the whirlwind with its own fans. Before the 2021 season began, I spoke to a writer named Matt Brown, who produces a newsletter called *Extra Points*. Brown is exceptionally well-informed and insightful about the business and culture of college sports, but unfortunately he also happens to be an OSU fan. He mentioned that he thought the Buckeye fan community would melt down to an unusual degree if the program ever became anything less than consistently dominant and that fans would specifically assert that the pensive Ryan Day's passing-heavy style of offense was a betrayal of the team's history as a tough Big Ten running team. This was exactly what happened in November. OSU fans were, and are, very, very mad about being "soft." As one poster on the Ohio State 247Sports site, Bucknuts, wrote, "When you go against a soft offense everyday [*sic*] in practice . . . your defense will be soft!! Period!!!" The subject line of that post? "Soft!!!!!"

Tim's friend Justin admitted that the win over Ohio State was "awesome."

The Twitter chat group, which had been named "The Soup Group" because of Iowa State's Matt "Soup" Campbell, was renamed "The Jim Group." **Thicc Stauskas** is concerned about the basketball team. "They're going to blow Mondo balls next year," he wrote recently, though he has changed his opinion about the matter several times since.

Jim Harbaugh interviewed for a job with the Minnesota Vikings after a month of rumors and reports about his interest in an NFL position, but he told members of the press immediately afterward he would be remaining as Michigan's head coach instead. In February 2022, he signed a new contract with Michigan and will now make about as much money annually as he used to. On ESPN, Paul Finebaum called the contract "preposterous," said Harbaugh had obviously not wanted to return to Michigan, and called the "optics" of the situation "really bad." The hot seat is dead; long live the hot seat.

REFERENCES

Adelson, Andrea, and David M. Hale. "Inside the 6-Year Unraveling of Florida State Football." ESPN.com. November 19, 2020. https://www .espn.com/college-football/story/_/id/30331494/deep-deep-hole -6-year-unraveling-florida-state-football.

Alberta, Tim. "The Senator Who Decided to Tell the Truth." *The Atlantic*, June 30, 2021. https://www.theatlantic.com/politics/archive/2021 /06/michigan-republican-truth-election-fraud/619326/.

Arsenault, Raymond. "The End of the Long Hot Summer: The Air Conditioner and Southern Culture." *Journal of Southern History* 50, no. 4 (November 1984): 597–628.

Auerbach, Nicole. "How College Football's Playoff-centricism Shows Up on TV, and How Broadcasters Are Trying to Fix It." The Athletic. June 15, 2021. https://theathletic.com/2651154/2021/06/15 /how-college-footballs-playoff-centric-parity-issue-shows-up-on -tv-and-how-broadcasters-are-trying-to-fix-it/.

Barra, Allen. "The Integration of College Football Didn't Happen in One Game." *The Atlantic*, November 15, 2013. https://www .theatlantic.com/entertainment/archive/2013/11/the-integration -of-college-football-didnt-happen-in-one-game/281557/.

Birrell, Susan. "Sport as Ritual: Interpretations from Durkheim to Goffman." *Social Forces* 60, no. 2 (December 1981): 354–376.

Birrell, Susan, and Peter Donnelly. "Reclaiming Goffman: Erving Goffman's Influence on the Sociology of Sport." In *Sport and Modern Social Theorists*, edited by Richard Giulianotti, 49–64. New York: Palgrave Macmillan, 2004.

Charles Baird papers, 1892–1933. Assorted letters. University of Michigan, Bentley Historical Library.

Cohan, Noah. *We Average Unbeautiful Watchers: Fan Narratives and the Reading of American Sports.* Lincoln: University of Nebraska Press, 2019.

Crisler, Herbert Orin "Fritz." *Modern Football: Fundamentals and Strategy.* New York: Whittlesey House, 1949.

Curtis, Bryan. "Sports Radio in the Age of Trump." The Ringer. November 22, 2016. https://www.theringer.com/2016/11/22/16038702/donald-trump-sports-radio-colin-cowherd-mike-francesa-190a7f57a543.

Dohrmann, George. "SI Investigation Reveals Eight-Year Pattern of Violations under Tressel." *Sports Illustrated*, May 30, 2011. https://www.si.com/more-sports/2011/05/31/jim-tressel.

Douglass, John Aubrey. "The Rise of the Publics: American Democracy, the Public University Ideal, and the University of California." Center for Studies in Higher Education Research and Occasional Papers Series, February 2018.

Eagleman, David. "The Moral of the Story." Review of *The Storytelling Animal*, by Jonathan Gottschall. *New York Times*, August 3, 2012. https://www.nytimes.com/2012/08/05/books/review/the-storytelling-animal-by-jonathan-gottschall.html.

Elliott, Bud. "Blue-Chip Ratio: Which College Football Teams Have Championship-Grade Recruiting?" SBNation. February 18, 2014. https://www.sbnation.com/college-football-recruiting/2014/2/18/5312840/college-football-recruiting-teams-championships.

Geertz, Clifford. "Deep Play: Notes on the Balinese Cockfight." *Daedalus* 101, no. 1 (Winter 1972): 1–38.

Gilbert, Jack. "A Brief for the Defense." *Refusing Heaven: Poems.* New York: Knopf, 2005.

Goffman, Erving. "On Cooling the Mark Out: Some Aspects of Adaptation to Failure." *Psychiatry* 15, no. 4 (1952): 451–463.

Hayes, Chris. "On the Internet, We're Always Famous." *New Yorker*, September 24, 2021. https://www.newyorker.com/news/essay/on-the-internet-were-always-famous.

Hochschild, Arlie Russell. *Strangers in Their Own Land: Anger and Mourning on the American Right.* New York: The New Press, 2016.

Kennedy, John F. "New England and the South." *The Atlantic*, January

1954. https://www.theatlantic.com/magazine/archive/1954/01
/new-england-and-the-south/376244/.

Koo, Ben. "College Football's Biggest Threat Is the Continued Region-
alization of Success and Interest in the Sport." Awful Announcing.
January 12, 2022. https://awfulannouncing.com/ncaa/college
-footballs-biggest-threat-is-the-continued-regionalization-of
-success-and-interest-in-the-sport.html.

Kuper, Simon. *Football Against the Enemy*. London: Trafalgar Square,
1994.

"LOUISIANA: Jimmy the Stooge." *Time*, July 10, 1939. https://content
.time.com/time/subscriber/article/0,33009,761630,00.html.

McIntire, Mike, and Walt Bogdanich. "At Florida State, Football Clouds
Justice." *New York Times*, October 10, 2014. https://www.nytimes
.com/2014/10/12/us/florida-state-football-casts-shadow-over
-tallahassee-justice.html.

Peckham, Howard H. *The Making of the University of Michigan
1817–1992 (175th anniversary edition)*. Ann Arbor: Bentley Historical Library, University of Michigan, 1994.

Pop, Iggy. "Caesar Lives." *Classics Ireland* 2 (1995): 94–96.

Public Sector Consultants. "Economic, Cultural, and Political History
of Michigan." In *Michigan in Brief: An Issues Handbook 2002–2003*.
Lansing, MI: Public Sector Consultants, 2002.

Schexnayder, C. J. "LSU vs. Auburn and 76 Years of SEC Saturday Nights
in Tiger Stadium." SBNation. October 21, 2011. https://www
.sbnation.com/ncaa-football/2011/10/21/2501372/lsu-auburn
-2011-night-games-series-history.

Schrotenboer, Brent. "LSU's Ed Orgeron Almost Got Kicked Off His College Team; Now He's a State Hero." *USA Today*, January 13, 2020.
https://www.usatoday.com/story/sports/ncaaf/2020/01/13/lsu
-coach-ed-orgeron-almost-got-kicked-off-his-college-football
-team/4431400002/.

Scott, Robert Travis. "The Enduring Mystery of Who Killed Huey P.
Long." *Times-Picayune*, September 5, 2010. https://www.nola.com
/news/politics/article_b997fc67-d3e8-5a86-803b-2e19a06e38e0
.html.

Smith, Douglas. "Presidential Myth: The Real Story of Gerald Ford, Willis
Ward and the 1934 Michigan / Georgia Tech Football Game." *Wash-*

tenaw Watchdogs. January 7, 2014. http://www.washtenawwatchdogs .com/the-real-story-of-gerald-ford-wilis-ward-and-the-1934 -michigan-georgia-tech-football-game/presidential-myth-the -real-story-of-gerald-ford-willis-ward-and-the-1934-michigan -georgia-tech-football-game.

Staples, Andy. "Moments of Truth: Ed Orgeron's Lifetime of Making Mistakes and Learning from Them Preps Him for Dream Job at LSU." *Sports Illustrated*, October 20, 2016. https://www.si.com /college/video/2016/11/29/moments-truth-ed-orgerons-lifetime -making-mistakes-and-learning-them-preps-him-dream-job-lsu.

Tarver, Erin C. *The I in Team: Sports Fandom and the Reproduction of Identity*. Chicago: University of Chicago Press, 2017.

Tarver, Erin C. "The Moral Equivalent of Football." *The Pluralist* 15, no. 2 (Summer 2020): 91–109.

Toma, J. Douglas. *Football U: Spectator Sports in the Life of the American University*. Ann Arbor: University of Michigan Press, 2003.

Walker, Mason. "U.S. Newsroom Employment Has Fallen 26% Since 2008." Pew Research Center, July 13, 2021. https://www.pewresearch .org/fact-tank/2021/07/13/u-s-newsroom-employment-has -fallen-26-since-2008/.

White, Derrick E. *Blood, Sweat, & Tears: Jake Gaither, Florida A&M, and the History of Black College Football*. Chapel Hill: University of North Carolina Press, 2019.

White, Derrick E. "From Desegregation to Integration: Race, Football, and 'Dixie' at the University of Florida." *Florida Historical Quarterly* 88, no. 4 (Spring 2010): 469–496.

WilmerHale. *Report of Independent Investigation: Allegations of Sexual Misconduct Against Robert E. Anderson*. May 11, 2021. https:// regents.umich.edu/files/meetings/01-01/WH_Anderson_Report .pdf.

ACKNOWLEDGMENTS

This book covers one season of college football, but it took an entire college playing career's worth of time (including a redshirt season) to make it happen. My thanks to my agent David Patterson—as well as to Aemilia Phillips and Chandler Wickers—at Stuart Krichevsky for sticking with it for the duration.

I wouldn't have conceived and written this book without MGoBlog and its staff, past and present. Thanks to Ace Anbender, Seth Fisher, and Brian Cook for pioneering the role of the critically independent fan-writer and for their willingness to entertain my persistent, obsessive questions. Thanks also to Spencer Hall and the Every Day Should Be Saturday diaspora for creating the academic subfield this book falls into—comparative college football as American studies, with regional-stereotype jokes.

I made constant requests for favors from other journalists and writers during this process. None of them had any ethical or personal obligation to help me, but they almost all did, with enthusiasm. Justin Rogers and Austin Meek gave me lay-of-the-land advice. Matt Brown, Richard Johnson, and Paul Putz are cited in the book as sources, but also answered follow-up questions and reviewed material while it was still being worked on. Tim Burke, Bill Connelly, and Bryan Curtis provided domain-specific expertise. John U. Bacon was preposterously gracious and helpful toward someone who was essentially working on a project whose tagline could have been "a John U. Bacon book, but weird."

Thanks to Michael Bonnette and Kaitlyn Vincek at LSU, Katrina McCormick and Kris Bartels at FAU, and Chad Shepard at Michigan for facilitating trips and interviews.

At PublicAffairs, Ben Adams's big-picture guidance and confidence were essential for a first-time author. Jennifer Crane did a superb, detailed job copy editing on a tight schedule. Elisa Rivlin did the same with the legal review. I've only just met Jocelynn Pedro and Miguel Cervantes, who are publicity and marketing experts. respectively, but I'm already enjoying it (and learning a lot). Thanks also to Pete Garceau and Spencer Fuller for their work on the book's design, in particular its outstanding cover, which I appreciate for being so perfect that I could be a chill, low-maintenance author and honestly respond, "It looks great to me, I have no suggestions!"

To the Soup Chat, what can I say but [parody] [redacted]? Thank you especially to Alex Cook, who, in addition to attending a game with me, read this entire manuscript to make sure it passed the "True Michigander" test, and to Connor Wroe Southard, for reviewing the sections of fancy ideas-talkin'.

Thanks to Tim, Brian, Adam, Josh, and Brad—the original gang. (Thanks especially to Tim for the lodging and companionship.) We finally danced the victory dance. Goooooo!

Thanks to the community of ethicists in the Gray Guide and to Amos Barshad, Ira Boudway, Sam Graham-Felsen, Seth Stevenson for commiseration on the writer's life. Thanks to Sam and Sasha Weiss, and to our neighbors Julia and Josh, for basically being my only social contacts for two-plus years. And thanks to Marc Tracy for thinking this book was not a terrible idea when I mentioned it to him in 2018!

Thanks also to the people who go way back: Nils Lundblad, Sarah Robinson, Emma Rosenblum, Julia Turner, my high school teachers (Don Demko, Amy Hutchinson, Carol Neff), and the

Wasserstein family, especially Ben Wasserstein—always my biggest advocate, who sees things for me well before I see them for myself and helps make them happen.

Thanks to my colleagues and former colleagues at Slate.com. My editors during the period I was researching and writing the book—Tom Scocca, Natalie Shutler, and Jordan Weissmann—were unnecessarily supportive of my bifurcated attention and random schedule needs. My colleagues on the politics team are very patient with my now-unshakeable tendency to analogize every event in American politics to something that happened in college football, a sport none of them follow. Allison Benedikt is a great editor, boss, friend, and role model for how to navigate an insane and dehumanizing industry/universe with the correct disposition and demeanor. She also read and suggested edits to the book's conclusion. But I didn't have to take them because she's not in charge of me anymore! Mwahaha! (I took them.)

Deservedly last in the non-family division here are Joel Anderson and Josh Levin. They gave this project a huge amount of support, both direct and indirect. From indulging my theories and questions in many, many direct messages, to giving advice on the seed of the idea that became the proposal, to being the first people I asked to explain what the South's "whole deal" is, to reading chapters despite their extremely active personal and professional lives, they were, like, the guardian angels of this book.

Finally, thanks to my family. Thank you to my mom and dad, Sue and Joe, for teaching me how to read and write and how to throw and catch. And to my in-laws, Carrie and Walter, for the childcare and for always maintaining a welcoming (and well-stocked) base of operations within driving range of Ann Arbor. Thank you to my wife Caroline, who made me consider being happy—and, of equal importance, did five years of life rearrangement, editorial and strategic consulting, and personal counseling related to this book. And thank you to our beautiful boy and girls Louie, Mirabel, and Beatrice. Well, guys, what's next?

Ben Mathis-Lilley is a senior writer for Slate.com, where he writes blog posts, columns, and feature stories about news, politics, and sports. He worked previously at *New York* magazine and, briefly but gloriously, as the editor of BuzzFeed's sports section. He lives in New Jersey.

PublicAffairs is a publishing house founded in 1997. It is a tribute to the standards, values, and flair of three persons who have served as mentors to countless reporters, writers, editors, and book people of all kinds, including me.

I. F. Stone, proprietor of *I. F. Stone's Weekly*, combined a commitment to the First Amendment with entrepreneurial zeal and reporting skill and became one of the great independent journalists in American history. At the age of eighty, Izzy published *The Trial of Socrates*, which was a national bestseller. He wrote the book after he taught himself ancient Greek.

Benjamin C. Bradlee was for nearly thirty years the charismatic editorial leader of *The Washington Post*. It was Ben who gave the *Post* the range and courage to pursue such historic issues as Watergate. He supported his reporters with a tenacity that made them fearless and it is no accident that so many became authors of influential, best-selling books.

Robert L. Bernstein, the chief executive of Random House for more than a quarter century, guided one of the nation's premier publishing houses. Bob was personally responsible for many books of political dissent and argument that challenged tyranny around the globe. He is also the founder and longtime chair of Human Rights Watch, one of the most respected human rights organizations in the world.

· · ·

For fifty years, the banner of Public Affairs Press was carried by its owner Morris B. Schnapper, who published Gandhi, Nasser, Toynbee, Truman, and about 1,500 other authors. In 1983, Schnapper was described by *The Washington Post* as "a redoubtable gadfly." His legacy will endure in the books to come.

[signature]

Peter Osnos, *Founder*